Nuclear Pacifism: 'Just War' Thinking Today

D1206494

American University Studies

Series VII
Theology and Religion

Vol. 4

PETER LANG
New York · Berne · Frankfort on the Main · Nancy

Edward J. Laarman

Nuclear Pacifism

'Just War' Thinking Today

PETER LANG
New York · Berne · Frankfort on the Main · Nancy

Library of Congress Cataloging in Publication Data

Laarman, Edward J., 1949–
  Nuclear pacifism.

  (American University Studies. Series VII, Theology
and religion; v. 4)
  Bibliography: p.
  1. Just war doctrine. 2. Atomic warfare – Religious
aspects – Christianity. 3. Atomic warfare – Moral and
ethical aspects. I. Title. II. Series.
  U21.2.L32   1984   261.8'73   84-47543
  ISBN 0-8204-0121-8
  ISSN 0740-0446

CIP-Kurztitelaufnahme der Deutschen Bibliothek

Laarman, Edward J.:
Nuclear pacifism: 'just war' thinking today /
Edward J. Laarman. – New York; Berne;
Frankfort on the Main; Nancy: Lang, 1984.
  (American University Studies: Ser. 7, Theo-
  logy and religion; Vol. 4)
  ISBN 0-8204-0121-8

NE: American University Studies / 07

© Peter Lang Publishing, Inc., New York 1984

Printed by Lang Druck Inc., Liebefeld/Berne (Switzerland)

ACKNOWLEDGMENTS

This manuscript was originally written as a dissertation. Upon its completion in 1982 I received a Ph.D. degree in Theological Ethics from the University of Notre Dame. Though it is the product of many lonely hours spent in the Memorial Library of Notre Dame, I could not have completed it without the help and support of many different people. First of all I want to thank my wife Joan. My graduate education and the beginning of my teaching career has given her many burdens and few rewards, yet she has shown a love, patience and cheerfulness that has amazed me over and over again. My two young sons Joel and Benjamin were also very helpful in relieving the intellectual and spiritual burdens of thinking about nuclear war. I am grateful to both my parents and my parents-in-law for their deep sense that God is at the center of life and therefore work in the field of theology is a worthy calling.

It has been my great privilege to work with John Howard Yoder during my years at Notre Dame. He has been instrumental in bringing me not only to a fuller pacifist commitment but also to an appreciation of the just war tradition. Though John Yoder's name seldom appears in these pages, I have learned so much from him that it seems ungrateful to call some of these thoughts my own. As a dissertation director Dr. Yoder was very helpful and accommodating, and I continue to value his friendship and wisdom.

Stanley Hauerwas as teacher, Graduate Director, and reader not only helped a great deal with the manuscript but always showed a warm interest in my progress as a student and now as a teacher. My other two dissertation readers, Fr. Edward Malloy, C.S.C., and Dr. Alan Dowty also deserve my thanks. Dr. Dowty both showed an interest in the ethical discussion of the nuclear issue and provided valuable strategic expertise.

Many other family members, friends, fellow students and teachers, and library personnel have helped me along the way. My typist Bobbi Thompson deserves special thanks. She not only worked expertly from a contorted, handwritten manuscript, but she arranged her schedule to meet my needs.

It has not been pleasant to write and think about nuclear war, but I have been buoyed by all of those who work and pray for peace.

Finally, as I think of all of these people, I can only thank God for them, and for each day of life and hope that He has given me.

I wish to thank the following for giving me permission to quote from copyrighted material:

Council on Religion and International Affairs: Modern War and the Pursuit of Peace by Theodore Weber, 1968; Peace, the Churches and the Bomb, edited by James Finn, 1965.

Merlin Press: Nuclear Weapons and Christian Conscience, edited by Walter Stein, 1961; reprinted in 1981 and currently available in paperback.

Paul Ramsey: The Just War: Force and Political Responsibility, copyright c 1968, 1983 by Paul Ramsey, University Press of America, Inc., 1983.

TABLE OF CONTENTS

LIST OF ABBREVIATIONS

Anscombe, "War and Murder": Anscombe, G.E.M. (Elizabeth). "War and Murder."
  In Nuclear Weapons and Christian Conscience, pp. 45-62. Edited by Walter
  Stein. London: Merlin Press, 1961.

Bloesch, "The Christian": Bloesch, Donald G. "The Christian and the Drift
  Towards War." Theology and Life, II (1959), 318-326.

Christian Approach: Christian Approach to Nuclear War, A. New York: Church
  Peace Mission, [1960]. Reprinted in Worldview, IV (1961), 3-7.

Crane, "Catholic": Crane, Paul. "Catholics and Nuclear War," The Month, New
  Series, XXII (1959), 223-229.

Ford, "Obliteration Bombing": Ford, John C. "The Morality of Obliteration
  Bombing," Theological Studies, V (1944), 261-309.

Ford and Winters, ENS?: Ford, Harold P. and Winters, Francis X. (eds.). Ethics
  and Nuclear Strategy? Maryknoll, N.Y.: Orbis Books, 1977.

Gessert and Hehir, NND: Gessert, Robert A. and Hehir, J. Bryan. The New Nuclear
  Debate. Special Studies No. 215. New York: The Council on Religion and
  International Affairs, 1976.

Gottwald, "NR or NP?": Gottwald, Norman K. "Nuclear Realism or Nuclear Pacifism?,"
  Christian Century, LXXVII (1960), 895-899.

Gottwald, "Reflections": Gottwald, Norman K. "Moral and Strategic Reflections on
  the Nuclear Dilemma," Christianity and Crisis, XXI (1962), 239-242.

McReavy, "Debate": McReavy, Lawrence L. "The Debate on the Morality of Future
  War," Clergy Review, VL (1960), 77-87.

McReavy, Peace: McReavy, Lawrence L. Peace and War in Catholic Doctrine. Oxford:
  Catholic Social Guild, 1963.

McReavy, "Reprisals": McReavy, Lawrence L. "Reprisals: A Second Opinion,"
  Clergy Review, XX (1941), 131-138.

Markus, "Conscience": Markus, R.A. "Conscience and Deterrence." In Nuclear
  Weapons and Christian Conscience, pp. 65-88. Edited by Walter Stein. London:
  Merlin Press, 1961.

Mohan, "Thermonuclear War": Mohan, Robert Paul. "Thermonuclear War and the
  Christian." In Christian Ethics and Nuclear Warfare. Edited by Ulrich S.
  Allers and William V. O'Brien. Washington, D.C.: Institute of World Polity,
  Georgetown University, 1963.

Morals and Missiles: Thompson, Charles S. (ed.). Morals and Missiles: Catholic
  Essays on the Problem of War Today. London: James Clarke Co. Ltd., 1959.

Murray, MMW: Murray, John Courtney. Morality and Modern War. New York: The
  Council on Religion and International Affairs, 1959.

Peace, Churches, Bomb: Finn, James (ed.). Peace, the Churches and the Bomb. New
  York: The Council on Religion and International Affairs, 1965.

Ramsey, Just War: Ramsey, Paul. The Just War: Force and Political Responsibility.
  New York: Charles Scribner's Sons, 1968.

Ramsey, WCC: Ramsey, Paul. War and the Christian Conscience: How Shall Modern
  War Be Conducted Justly? Durham, N.C.: Duke University Press, 1961.

Ryan, "Modern War": Ryan, John K. "Modern War and Basic Ethics." Doctoral
  dissertation. Catholic University of America, 1933.

Stein, NWCC: Stein, Walter (ed.). Nuclear Weapons and Christian Conscience.
  London: Merlin Press, 1961. Published in the United States as Nuclear Weapons
  A Catholic Response. New York: Sheed and Ward, 1961.

Stein, Peace on Earth: Stein, Walter (ed.). Peace on Earth: The Way Ahead. London
  and Melbourne: Sheed and Ward, 1966.

Watkin, "Unjustifiable War": Watkin, E.I. "Unjustifiable War." In Morals and
  Missiles: Catholic Essays on the Problem of War Today, pp. 51-62. Edited
  by Charles Thompson. London: James Clarke Co., Ltd., 1959.

Weber, MWPP: Weber, Theodore. Modern War and the Pursuit of Peace. New York:
  The Council on Religion and International Affairs, 1968.

Chapter I

THE DEBATE ABOUT MODERN WARFARE

Throughout history few human activities have been celebrated and
denounced as much as warfare: celebrated as the arena of the gods, the
gateway to empire, the showcase of courage, and the source of power,
glory, and wealth; denounced as utter sacrilege, the ruin of nations and
peoples, the triumph of cruelty, and the messenger of poverty, despair
and death.

Between these poles of attitude there is room for an infinite variety
of thought about war within particular traditions. In the Hebrew scriptures there are accounts of holy war under Joshua, the laws of war given
to Moses (Deuteronomy 20), Jeremiah's call to surrender to Babylon, and
the prophets' visions of peace. Jews today range from militarists to
pacifists, with most falling somewhere in between. The Christian New
Testament appears on the face of it to be pacifistic and for the first
three centuries the Christian church was predominantly pacifist. After
that Ambrose, Augustine and others led in adopting the Greco-Roman tradition of the just war, especially as mediated by Cicero, for use in the
church as part of the "Constantinian change". Through the centuries a
body of thought developed particularly by the exercise of casuistry, the
process of making judgments about issues and events concerning warfare.
The medieval crusade raised new issues but the just war ethic was
thought to encompass all wars whether waged for religious or political
purposes. Only after the end of the post-Reformation religious wars did

the theory (if not always the mentality) of war waged for religious purposes fade from the just war tradition.

The just war tradition[1] has three basic purposes: 1) To justify participation in warfare. Since there is a prima facie duty not to kill, reason must be given for justifying it as an exception to the rule. That reason is that in a sinful world warfare is sometimes necessary to preserve order, justice, and security. It follows therefore that only those wars which in intention and fact serve these goals may be justified as exceptions to the rule. Thus the second purpose of the tradition is: 2) To distinguish between wars which are justified and those which are not. Because only just and necessary violence may be permitted even in a justified war (except possibly in the case of a crusade), there is a third goal: 3) To limit the evil effects of war.

The way in which twentieth century Christians, particularly Roman Catholics, have received the tradition in regard to the second and third purposes is a list of criteria distilled from earlier thought. Such a form was used at least as far back as Thomas Aquinas (Summa Theologiae II-II, Q. 40, art. 1). The criteria are used to judge whether or not a particular war is just and whether the means employed in warfare are just. There is no standard list, but criteria commonly included today are: 1) Legitimate authority: only rulers may declare war. 2) Just cause: war may be waged only for defense against aggression, the punishment of

---

[1] The word "tradition" is preferred to "theory" when applied generally because it has been variously formulated in history. Cf. LeRoy Walters, "Five Classic Just-War Theories: A Study in the Thought of Thomas Aquinas, Vitoria, Suarez, Gentili, and Grotius," (Unpublished doctoral dissertation, Yale University, 1971), p. 420.

guilt (more traditional than current), or the recovery of property/ securing of violated rights. 3) Right intention: the goal must be to secure peace and justice, not power and wealth, and the attitude cannot be one of cruelty. 4) Due means: the innocent (non-combatants) are immune from direct attack; any punishment inflicted must be proportionate to guilt: the good and evil effects of any military action must be proportionate; captives must be properly treated; no unnecessary harm must be inflicted; and so forth. 5) Proportionality of good and evil: the war must produce more good or avoid more evil than it causes. 6) There must be reasonable hope of victory (winability): it is useless to fight a war that will be lost (though sometimes exceptions are made to this rule). 7) The war must be waged according to what may be called "due form": war must be a last resort, there must be a formal declaration of war, there must be respect for international conventions of warfare.

The chief bearer of the Christian just war tradition in its most detailed form has been the Roman Catholic Church. Since the Reformation most Protestant groups have also endorsed the doctrine but have generally been less clear about the criteria and less inclined to casuistry based on them. After being relatively neglected for two or three centuries, the tradition has since World War II both enjoyed renewed interest and suffered unprecedented challenges. Both the destructive power of modern weapons and the development of guerrilla warfare have challenged the relevance and integrity of the just war tradition. In this study I will examine a new position on war which has emerged in this century: "nuclear pacifism", which affirms the just war tradition but concludes that the nature of at least some modern weapons is such that any war in which they were used would be unjust. Toward the end of the chapter I will define that view more carefully, but first I will describe some of the military and political developments of the nuclear era and a few international Christian statements on nuclear weapons.

The Advent of Nuclear Weapons

Warfare as the organized, collective use of violence against another group has been known throughout history. Its form has varied between cultures and historical periods according to different forms of social organization, technology, religious and philosophical values, and so forth. In the judgment of many one of the most radical changes in warfare occurred in the twentieth century with the advent of "total war." Whereas in European history war had been primarily a contest between rulers and designated classes of soldiers, although of course the entire population might be affected in various ways, "a total war is one in which an entire society wages war on another society".[2] All classes of society are urged to give moral support to the war effort, particularly if it has an ideological tint, and soldiers are drawn from all groups. Also because war is more mechanized it is not only more destructive but it requires the mobilization of economic and other institutions at a higher level than before. Because of these factors the whole population of the opposing side has come to be seen as a potential target. It was especially the development of the airplane that made the potential an actuality. No longer was battle limited to the front, for war could be carried behind enemy lines. In total war too the objective is the "unconditional surrender" of the enemy.

The beginnings of total war were evidenced already in the Napoleanic Wars, the American Civil War, and World War I, but it reached its height in World War II. Germany engaged in heavy bombing early in the war, but

---

[2] William O'Brien, Nuclear War, Deterrence and Morality, (New York, 1967), p. 5.

in 1942 England and the United States began to adopt a policy of "obliteration bombing" in which whole areas of cities were destroyed in an effort to break the morale of the German people as much as to destroy Germany's military and industrial capacity.[3] The destruction of Hamburg, Dresden and Tokyo were only the most notorious examples of this policy. When the atom bomb was dropped on Hiroshima and Nagasaki it showed a technological breakthrough but a continuation of established practice. Whereas the very biggest "blockbuster" bombs of World War II contained ten to twenty tons of TNT, the bombs dropped on Japan were 1,000 times more powerful for they had a destructive force of twelve to twenty kilotons (a kiloton is equivalent to 1,000 tons of TNT).[4] It was now possible to accomplish with one bomb what it took thousands of bombs to do earlier in the war. But less than ten years later even the atomic bomb was dwarfed by the hydrogen bomb, which may have destructive power measured by the megaton: the equivalent of one million tons of TNT.[5]

As the "Cold War" set in after World War II, the West regarded atomic bombs as a balance to the conventional power of the larger communist land armies, though the Soviet Union itself developed the bomb by 1949.[6] It

---

[3] E.g. Guenter Lewy, "Superior Orders, Nuclear Warfare, and the Dictates of Conscience: The Dilemma of Military Obedience in the Atomic Age," Political Science Review, LV (1961), 14; Vera Brittain, Seed of Chaos: What Mass Bombing Really Means (London, 1944).

[4] David Inglis, "The Nature of Nuclear War," Nuclear Weapons and the Conflict of Conscience, ed. John C. Bennett (New York, 1962), p. 42.

[5] The destructive power of the atomic bomb results from atomic fission; that of the hydrogen or "thermonuclear" bomb, from atomic fusion. Henceforth unless otherwise specified I will use the word "nuclear" for all weapons using the power of the atom.

[6] William McFadden, "A Theological Evaluation of Nuclear Pacifism as Held by Selected Christian Thinkers," (Unpublished doctoral dissertation, Boston University, 1966), p. 1.

was particularly the Korean conflict which led Secretary of State John Foster Dulles to spell out the United States policy for deterring communist aggression, as described for instance in his article "Policy for Security and Peace" (Foreign Affairs, April, 1954, pp. 353-364). His central point was that aggression could be deterred by a "collective system of defense" which could retaliate on a level unacceptable to any aggressor. Since the West could not afford to match the manpower of the Soviet-Chinese bloc, it should emphasize its assets of air and naval power and "atomic weapons which are now available in a wide range, suitable not only for strategic bombing but also for extensive tactical use" (pp. 357-358).[7] He threatened to extend the war if the communists violated the armistice in Korea, though he preferred to keep them uncertain about whether that would mean "atomic warfare throughout Asia" (p. 360) or something less. Dulles stressed flexibility but the policy was based ultimately on the threat of "massive atomic and thermonuclear retaliation" (p. 356). The targets of such retaliation by atom and hydrogen bombs he

---

[7] The distinction between tactical and strategic nuclear weapons is not precise, but in general tactical nuclear weapons are intended for battlefield use, have less destructive power, and are of shorter range. Strategic nuclear weapons are generally of longer range and are targeted on the homeland of the potential enemy. It should be remembered that the distinction is relative. In 1957 Reinhold Niebuhr commended the idea of Henry Kissinger's new book, Nuclear Weapons and Foreign Policy, that war with ultimate weapons is suicidal so we must be prepared to fight limited nuclear war. "Limited Warfare," Christianity and Crisis, November 11, 1957, pp. 146-147. He was shocked to learn shortly afterwards that "tactical" weapons are approximately the size of the Nagasaki bomb and he wondered whether Kissinger knew this when he recommended tactical weapons "with seeming equanimity". Reinhold Niebuhr, "The Moral Insecurity of Our Security," Christianity and Crisis, January 6, 1958, p. 177. However, as we will note in the next chapter some nuclear weapons much smaller than this were soon added to the tactical arsenal. The Glossary of Christian Ethics and Nuclear Warfare, ed. Ulrich Allers and William O'Brien (Washington, 1963), pp. 55, 56, says that generally tactical nuclear weapons are defined as those with yields of 20 kilotons or under; strategic weapons, 50 kilotons or more.

described only as "the war industries of an attacking nation" (p. 356) and "the great industrial centers of China or Russia" (p. 359). Dulles did not spell out whether this policy included the actual targeting of cities per se, but later officials expressly threatened, in the words of President Eisenhower, the "virtual annihilation" of the country of any attacker.[8]

One of the drawbacks of this vague policy of "massive retaliation" was that it gave no guidelines by which to establish how many weapons were enough. In the 1960's under American Secretary of Defense Robert McNamara, the prevailing idea was that the ability to kill immediately (not counting deaths from fall-out and so forth) about 25 percent of the Soviet population and 50-60 percent of its industry would be a sufficient deterrent to the Soviet Union, and only enough weapons were needed to accomplish this purpose. Because of these limits the policy could be called one of "finite" or "minimum" deterrence.[9] "Minimum" of course did not mean "small", for the policy threatened the "assured destruction" of any enemy who launched a nuclear attack. However, such a threat would only be an effective deterrent if it could be inflicted even after a massive "first strike" by the Soviet Union. Thus as technology advanced, land-based intercontinental ballistic missiles and submarine-launched ballistic missiles were added to strategic bombers to form the "Strategic Triad." Each leg of this triad was supposed to be able to accomplish the desired

---

[8]Quoted along with similar statements by Walter Stein, "Would You Press the Button?". Peace, the Churches and the Bomb, ed. James Finn (New York, 1965), p. 21. This is a symposium by John Wright, Theodore Weber, Walter Stein, William O'Brien, Justus George Lawler, and Paul Ramsey. Hereafter cited as Peace, Churches, Bomb along with the author being quoted.

[9]Fred Kaplan, Dubious Specter: A Skeptical Look at the Soviet Nuclear Threat (Washington, D.C., 1980), pp. 2-5. Hereafter cited as Kaplan, Dubious Specter. It was calculated that about 500 megatons would meet the stated goals of destruction.

destruction independently, and together they were to provide an invulner-able "second-strike" capability.[10]

On a more limited scale, Great Britain and France also developed independent nuclear deterrents based on the ability to assure unacceptable damage to the Soviet Union. Of course, in the 1950's and 1960's the Soviet Union was also developing its nuclear arsenal. The deterrence policy of "assured destruction" was formulated in the context of "mutual assured destruction" or "MAD" as some, especially critics of the policy, have been wont to call it.

While in itself the MAD policy might seem militaristic enough, it has actually tended to be a "dovish" position. Many "doves" favored the MAD policy because they saw it as the best way to preserve peace in the world. They wanted the prospect of nuclear war to remain so awful that no nation would initiate war, particularly nuclear war. Furthermore, they believed that as long as each side felt secure in its ability to inflict unaccep-table retaliation upon the enemy, the MAD policy could provide a stable, balanced system of deterrence. Thus there would be little need for addi-tional, more destructive, and more sophisticated weapons, and there would be a basis on which to reach agreements for mutual disarmament.

However, the MAD policy has not gone unchallenged in the last two decades. The targeting of cities and industrial capacity is called "countervalue" targeting, and the challenge has come from those advocating an emphasis on "counterforce" targeting against military targets. Attempts to emphasize the latter policy may be represented by three events. In June, 1962, Secretary of Defense Robert McNamara in a speech at the Uni-versity of Michigan advocated the development of conventional forces

---

[10]Ibid., p. 3.

<u>and</u> some shift from countervalue to counterforce targeting of nuclear weapons. A great deal of controversy developed, however, and "By the end of the decade that Ann Arbor speech was almost totally forgotten or repudiated."[11] Fear of upsetting the MAD deterrent system was instrumental in the defeat of the Sentinel anti-ballistic missile (ABM) defense systems proposed by President Johnson in 1967 and the Safeguard ABM proposed by President Nixon in 1969.[12] The SALT (Strategic Arms Limitation Treaty) I Anti-Ballistic Missile Treaty implicitly helped to establish MAD as the basic policy of both the U.S. and the U.S.S.R., since neither country was allowed to defend its territory with ABM's.[13]

A second attempt to deemphasize countervalue targeting was made by Secretary of Defense James Schlesinger in the Spring of 1974. He favored a shift from reliance on MAD to "selective response options" which would include counterforce targeting, along with the new and more powerful weapons that would be necessary for effective counterforce strikes. Schlesinger spoke partially in response to the perception of Soviet initiatives of increased targeting (particularly counterforce targeting), the defensive strengthening ("hardening") of their missile silos, and the increased ability of their warheads to destroy "hard" targets.[14]

---

[11]Gessert in Robert A. Gessert and J. Bryan Hehir, <u>The New Nuclear Debate</u> (New York, 1976), p. 13. Hereafter cited as Gessert and Hehir, <u>NND</u>.

[12]<u>Ibid.</u>, p. 8.

[13]Herbert Scoville, Jr., "Flexible MADness? The Case Against Counterforce," <u>Ethics and Nuclear Strategy</u>, ed. Harold Ford and Francis Winters (Maryknoll, N.Y., 1977), p. 114. The book will hereafter be cited as Ford and Winters, <u>ENS?</u>.

[14]Gessert and Hehir, <u>NND</u>, p. 25. The fact that Schlesinger requested new, more powerful and more sophisticated weapons provides a good example of the fact that counterforce policy is associated with an arms build-up.

The third event in this line is President Carter's Presidential Directive 59, which became public in August, 1980. Among other things it deemphasized major strikes against cities in favor of precise, limited attacks on military targets and the Soviet political leadership.[15]

These issues of military doctrine were of course interwoven with debates about particular weapons systems and domestic and foreign political issues which I cannot fully chronicle here. Also it might be debated just how much the targeting of the United States strategic deterrent actually shifted in the course of the countervalue/counterforce debates. It must be remembered first of all that even those officials who advocated counterforce targeting never withdrew the ultimate threat of countervalue retaliation.[16] Secondly, those who favored the policy of assured destruction never made it the sole military or

---

[15]Robert Gessert, "P.D. 59: The Better Way," Worldview, November, 1980, p. 7.

[16]This is at least true in the case of Robert McNamara, who in his Ann Arbor speech said that the NATO alliance would have, "even in the face of a massive surprise attack, sufficient reserve striking power to destroy an enemy society if driven to it." Robert S. McNamara, "The United States and Western Europe," Vital Speeches of the Day, XXVIII (1962), 628. Fred Kaplan in Dubious Specter, p. 8, quotes two statements from Carter administration leaders which throw into question whether they maintained this ultimate threat. On the other hand, Robert Gessert assumes that Schlesinger and Harold Brown, President Carter's Secretary of Defense, maintained the countercity threat as a last resort just as did McNamara. Robert Gessert, "P.D. 59: The Better Way," Worldview, November, 1980, p. 9. Also, first-term Congressman John P. Hiler, a Republican from the Third District of Indiana, wrote to me that "In the past 20 years, America's strategic nuclear policy has been linked to two basic beliefs. The first being that the perceived ability to inflict massive damage on an enemy following a nuclear strike on the United States would be sufficient to deter such a strike, and secondly, that a triad of offensive nuclear capabilities, including long-range bombers, land-based missiles, and missile-firing submarines would enable the United States to withstand a well-executed nuclear attach and deliver a fatal counterblow." John p. Hiler to Edward Laarman, October 29, 1981. However, Congressmen Hiler is probably not a military expert.

even strategic option. We have noted that Dulles emphasized flexibility
and ambiguity. Fred Kaplan claims that even though McNamara dropped the
counterforce rhetoric after his Ann Arbor speech the Pentagon continued to
pursue a counterforce strategy; it was only the Soviet strategic build-up
that later forced Schlesinger to bring the counterforce strategy out into
the open.[17] In summary we can simply say that while emphasis has shifted
back and forth between countervalue and counterforce targeting, no
option has been clearly and publicly repudiated in United States strategic
policy.

Despite the many changes in the complex strategic discussion of the
last twenty years, some themes have recurred constantly in the debate
between those favoring the MAD countervalue policy and those favoring
emphasis on the counterforce option. Critics of MAD makes these points:
1) If nuclear war is made so "unthinkable", the threat of it becomes
"unbelievable." There must be ways of fighting more limited wars so that
the nuclear arsenal will actually function as a deterrent. This issue
has been particularly acute in the case of Europe since the Soviet Union
developed the ability to threaten the continental United States with its
nuclear weapons. Is it really credible, ask these critics, that the
United States will risk its own destruction by retaliating against the
Soviet Union for Soviet advances in Europe? Therefore they favor the
readiness to use tactical nuclear weapons in battle there if necessary.[18]
2) The MAD policy relies totally on deterrence, but if deterrence fails,

---

[17] Kaplan, Dubious Specter, pp. 10-11.

[18] NATO adopted Dulles' doctrine of massive retaliation in 1957 but
changed to a policy of "flexible response" or "graduated deterrence" in
1967 to reflect the development of a Soviet "counterdeterrent to the U.S.
threat of retaliation." Robert Gessert in Gessert and Hehir, NND, pp.
81-82.

we have no options other than surrender or all-out nuclear war. Therefore we must seek ways to keep nuclear war limited if it does occur. This
is especially true because nuclear war can be initiated by accident, miscalculation, irrational behavior, or the actions of third parties. 3)
It is wrong to attack civilian populations, at least before all other
options have been employed. 4) MAD is not as stable a system as claimed;
we must be free to seek technological breakthrough and to respond to
changes in Soviet weaponry and policy. (Some would also seek to maintain
superiority over rather than parity with the Soviet Union.) 5) Regardless of strategic considerations, there are political advantages to being
perceived by the world as being able to attack Soviet forces.

The proponents of assured destruction make these counter-claims:
1) Our highest priority must be to prevent (nuclear) war, not to prepare
to fight it. 2) The talk of limited war only conceals the fact that no
one can "win" a nuclear war. Even the "limited" war envisaged would be
enormously destructive, and very probably it could not be limited any-
way. Nuclear war is only made more likely by minimizing its destructiveness. 3) Counterforce targeting encourages a first strike, since it is
useless to destroy an empty missile silo. This in turn encourages a
preemptive strike by the other side in times of tension. 4) The abandon-
ment of MAD threatens international stability, fosters an arms race, and
reduces prospects for arms control.

I have described some of the central events and issues in the development of the nuclear weapons arsenals of the West and particularly of the
United States. The strategic debate forms the background of and partially
overlaps with the religious debate that parallels it.

The Teaching of Recent Popes and the Second Vatican Council

Before focusing on British and American nuclear pacifism particularly, it would be well to survey wider Christian thought on the matter since World War II. However, even to review the literature of one country would require a dissertation in itself, particularly in countries such as Germany, the Netherlands, France, England, and the United States which have at least at times been quite concerned about the issue of nuclear weapons. Therefore I will instead briefly describe some of the statements of the Roman Catholic hierarchy and a few of the documents of the World Council of Churches from World War II to the 1960's. This will give some orientation to international thought on the matter and of course the teaching of the hierarchy is especially important because of the authority it has for Roman Catholics and to a lesser extent other Christians as well.

Pope Pius XII occupied the Holy See during World War II and throughout his reign never failed to stress the need to avoid war and build a peaceful international order. In the face of the vastly increased violence of modern war, he prohibited all war of aggression.[19] While the right of defense was maintained, it could be exercised only for grave reason, and "When the harm wrought by war is not comparable to that caused by 'tolerating injustice,' one may be obliged to 'suffer injustice'."[20] Pius XII was particularly horrified by atomic, bacteriological and chemical warfare, and he answered the question of whether their use

---

[19]Pope Pius XII, "The Doctor's Role in War and Peace," The Pope Speaks, I (1954), 349, 355.
[20]Ibid., p. 355.

could ever be permissible in this way:

> One cannot even in principle ask whether
> atomic, chemical, and bacteriological war-
> fare is lawful other than when it is deemed
> absolutely necessary as a means of self-
> defense under the conditions previously
> stipulated. Even then, however, every pos-
> sible effort must be made to avert it through
> international agreements, or to place upon
> its use such distinct and rigid limitations
> as will guarantee that its effects will be
> confined to the strict demands of defense.
> Moreover, should the use of this method en-
> tail such an extension of the existing evil
> as would render man wholly incapable of con-
> trolling it, its use should be rejected as
> immoral. In such an instance it would no
> longer be a question of "defense" against in-
> justice, and of the necessary "safeguarding" of
> legitimate possessions, but of the pure and
> simple annihilation of all human life within
> the radius of action. Under no circumstances is
> this to be permitted.[21]

Nuclear pacifists are prone to stress the criterion of control, which they believe nuclear warfare cannot meet, while their critics prefer to stress that the Pope did not close the door on the use of even these weapons. He did close the door on conscientious objection by Catholics in cases when a government legitimately enters a defensive war.[22]

Probably no Pope in recent times has more passionately stressed the theme of peace than John XXIII. In his encyclical _Pacem in Terris_[23] he called for an end to the arms race, the banning of nuclear weapons, and

---

[21] Ibid., p. 349.

[22] Pope Pius XII, "The Contradiction of Our Age" (Christmas Message, 1956), _The Pope Speaks_, III (1956-57), 343.

[23] Available for instance in David O'Brien and Thomas Shannon, ed., _Renewing the Earth: Catholic Documents on Peace, Justice and Liberation_ (Garden City, N.Y., 1977). pp. 124-170.

a program of progressive disarmament, all based on mutual trust and
accomplished by the coordinated action of all the nations concerned
(paras. 112 and 113). Like Pius XII, he called for the establishment of
a functional world-wide public authority to promote the universal common
good (paras. 136 and 137). Unlike Pius XII, he did not explicitly affirm
the interim right of states to fight a war of self-defense. A crucial
question here is the translation of a sentence in paragraph 127. The
translation authorized by the Vatican reads: "It is hardly possible to
imagine that in the atomic era wars could be used as an instrument of
justice."[24] This would seem to imply nuclear pacifism and has been
interpreted as such by Catholic pacifists and nuclear pacifists.[25] However, the translation in The Pope Speaks reads: "Thus, in this age which
boasts of its atomic power, it no longer makes sense to maintain that
war is a fit instrument with which to repair the violation of justice."[26]
Non-nuclear pacifists prefer this translation and interpret it as for-
bidding only aggressive war, not wars of self-defense, in which even the
controlled use of nuclear weapons may be allowed.[27]

The Second Vatican Council also addressed the issue of modern war.
Schema XIII, an early draft of its statement, concluded that while it

---

[24] Quoted in Paul Ramsey, The Just War: Force and Political
Responsibility (New York, 1968), p. 193. Hereafter cited as Ramsey,
Just War.

[25] Gerard Vanderhaar, "The Morality of Nuclear Deterrence," Cross
Currents, XXIX (1979-80), 412; James W. Douglass, The Non-Violent Cross:
A Theology of Revolution and Peace (London, 1966), pp. 84-85. In fact,
Douglas believes that Pope John was opposed to war in any form.

[26] The Pope Speaks, IX (1963), 38.

[27] Ramsey, The Just War, p. 193; James Dougherty, "The Christian and
Nuclear Pacifism," Catholic World, CXCVIII (1964), 342.

may at times be licit for a country to defend its rights by force, "nevertheless the use of arms, especially nuclear weapons, whose effects are greater than can be imagined and therefore cannot be reasonably regulated by men, exceeds all just proportion and therefore must be judged before God and man as most wicked."[28]

This wording, if not the conclusion, was changed in _Gaudium et Spes_ (_Pastoral Constitution on the Church in the Modern World_).[29] The Council did explicitly affirm that "as long as the danger of war persists and there is no international authority with the necessary competence and power, governments cannot be denied the right of lawful self-defense, once all peace efforts have failed." (Para. 79)[30] However, in view of the horrors of modern warfare the Bishops called for "a completely fresh appraisal of war" (para. 80), and for the first time acknowledged the rights of conscientous objectors (para. 79). In the strongest condemnation found in any of the Vatican II documents, the council stated:

> With these considerations in mind the Council, endorsing the condemnations of total warfare issued by recent popes, declares: Every act of war directed to the indiscriminate destruction of whole cities or vast areas with their inhabitants is a crime against God and man, which merits firm and unequivocal condemnation. (Para. 80)

---

[28] Quoted in _Peace, Churches, Bomb_, p. 102.

[29] Douglass, _op. cit._, p. 105, states that the Council switched from the technical criterion of "controllability" to the moral criterion of discrimination in order to avoid being challenged by defense experts.

[30] Quotations are from Austin Flannery, ed., _Documents of Vatican II_ (Grand Rapids, Michigan, 1975), pp. 986-993.

J. Bryan Hehir says of this statement: "It certainly is a prohibition of the use of _strategic_ nuclear weapons. Whether it can be said to be a definitive position of nuclear pacifism, condemning _all_ use of nuclear weapons, is less certain."[31]

On the issue of deterrence the Council did not render a clear judgment. Immediately after the statement quoted above it was noted that the possession of modern weapons exposed men to the risk of perpetrating such crimes and worse. However in the next paragraph (81) the Council recognized that armaments are "not amassed merely for use in wartime" but act "as a deterrent to potential attackers," and that "Many people look upon this as the most effective way known at the present time for maintaining some sort of peace among nations." "Whatever one may think of this form of deterrent," the statement concludes, the arms race does not lead to real peace. Therefore the Council went on to call for an end to the arms race, multilateral (not unilateral) disarmament and the establishment of a universal public authority so that all war might "be completely outlawed by international agreement" (para. 82).

In the following years Pope Paul VI continued to express these themes.[32]

---

[31] J. Bryan Hehir, "The Just-War Ethic and Catholic Theology: Dynamics of Change and Continuity," War or Peace? The Search for New Answers, ed. Thomas Shannon (Maryknoll, N.Y., 1980), p. 27. Paul Ramsey denies that the use of all nuclear weapons is condemned, but he does not make the strategic/tactical distinction. Ramsey, Just War, pp. 372, 376.

[32] E.g., Pope Paul VI, Address to the United Nations General Assembly, October 4, 1965, in The Gospel of Peace and Justice, ed. Joseph Gremillion (Maryknoll, N.Y., 1976), pp. 379-386; "Casting Out the Demons of War," Address to the United Nations General Assembly Special Session on Disarmament, June 6, 1978, Origins, VIII (1978), 69-72.

In summary, these statements of the Roman Catholic hierarchy show both a line of continuity and a line of development. The line of continuity is that of horror at the evil of modern war, condemnation of the dangerous and immorally expensive arms race, exhortation for the building of international trust, cooperation and peace, and hope for world organization to insure peace and justice. The line of development is one of increasing skepticism about the morality of the use of nuclear weapons and new awareness of the question of deterrence. As we will see in later chapters, these themes have been further developed by the American bishops in recent years.

Modern War and the World Council of Churches

There is of course no central Protestant authority comparable to the Popes and the Vatican Council. The nearest thing to it is the World Council of Churches, which does not even represent all Protestant groups and which also includes the Orthodox churches. In this section I will briefly survey a few documents of the World Council which focus on the issue of the morality of modern warfare.

The report of the First Assembly of the World Council of Churches in 1948 stated:

> Warfare has greatly changed. War is now total
> and every man and woman is called for mobilization
> in war service. Moreover, the immense use of
> air forces and the discovery of atomic and other
> new weapons render widespread and indiscriminate
> destruction inherent in the whole conduct of
> modern war in a sense never experienced in past
> conflicts. In these circumstances the tradition
> of a just war, requiring a just cause and the use
> of just means, is now challenged.[33]

The Assembly found itself unable to agree on an answer to the question, "Can war now be an act of Justice?" Three broad groups were identified: pacifists, those who consider war as a duty in defense of law, and "those who hold that, even though entering a war may be a Christian's duty in particular circumstances, modern warfare, with its mass destruction, can never be an act of justice."[34] The last statement does not seem to indicate what came to be called "nuclear pacifism" because participation

---

[33]First Assembly of the World Council of Churches, Report of Section IV, "The Church and the International Disorder," Part I; reprinted in Donald Durnbaugh, ed., On Earth Peace (Elgin, Illinois, 1978), p. 40. The book is hereafter cited as Durnbaugh, On Earth Peace.

[34]Ibid.

in unjust war is sometimes a duty,[35] but there is basis for the nuclear pacifist position in the recognition of the incompatibility of modern war and justice. The report recommended among other things "the multi-lateral reduction of armaments" and support for international law and international institutions, including the strengthening of the United Nations.[36]

In the final report of the Second General Assembly at Evanston in 1954, the three categories were collapsed to two, pacifists and those who hold that military action is justifiable in certain circumstances. While the right of national self-defense was recognized, it was stated that "the churches must condemn the deliberate mass destruction of civilians in open cities by whatever means and for whatever purpose."[37]

Further study of the issue of nuclear weapons was promoted when in 1955 the Central Committee of the World Council of Churches appointed a commission of fourteen European and American members, both theologians and non-theologians. In 1958 they produced their report entitled, Christians and the Prevention of War in the Atomic Age--A Theological Discussion.[38] Chapter I states that there are two dominant facts about war in the

---

[35]Ralph Potter, War and Moral Discourse (Richmond, Virginia, 1969), p. 113, is mistaken in calling this statement "nuclear pacifism", though perhaps nuclear pacifists were included in this group. Durnbaugh labels the statement, war as "an unjust necessity." On Earth Peace, p. 38.

[36]First Assembly, op. cit., Part III, pp. 42-43.

[37]Second Assembly of the World Council of Churches, Report of Section IV, "International Affairs--Christians in the Struggle for World Community," Evanston Speaks (New York, 1954), p. 40.

[38]World Council of Churches, Division of Studies, A Provisional Study Document on "Christians and the Prevention of War in an Atomic Age--A Theological Discussion," 1958.

present situation. The first is the existence and means of delivery of
the H-bomb. All-out war with such weapons would mean indiscriminate
destruction in which no political objective such as order or freedom
could be preserved. Such a war would be uncontrollable in space and
time because of fallout throughout the world and because of the genetic
effects on future generations. The second fact is the hostility between
the Communist and the non-Communist world. Chapter II calls Christians
to respond to this situation not according to a set of rules but according to a discipline of penitence, hope, faith, wisdom, obedience, and
love. The thesis of Chapter III is that there must be spiritual discipline to control the use of science and technology. Chapter IV enjoins
political discipline to produce an attitude of self-criticism by all
nations, the restrained use of power, the search for peaceful resolution
of international conflict, and the development of international law and
a strong world authority.

In Chapter V the report makes specific recommendations in regard to
warfare, and here the commission itself is divided into three groups
(cf. Preface, p. 17). One minority group is pacifist and another
minority group rejects any use or possession of hydrogen bombs. The
majority is more conservative but among its recommendations are two
which it knows to be controversial. The first is as follows:

> Although there are differences of opinion on many
> points, we are agreed on one point. This is that
> Christians should openly declare that the all-out
> use of these weapons should never be resorted to.
> Moreover, that Christians must oppose all policies
> which give evidence of leading to all out war.
> Finally, if all out war should occur, Christians
> should urge a cease fire, if necessary on the
> enemy's terms, and resort to non-violent resistence.
> We purposely refrain from defining the stage at
> which all out war may be reached. (para. 66)

According to para. 79, it is not necessary for a nation or group of
nations to announce in advance at what point it will stop fighting
rather than embark on all out war, because "This might tempt a hard
pressed enemy to test that point." (para. 79) A reservation by some
members of the Commission is interjected in paras. 69a, b, c, and d,
to the effect that because the H-bomb would kill immense numbers of
people indiscriminately, both combatants and non-combatants, it must
never under any circumstances be used (and by the same measure the use
of the atomic bomb and the aerial bombardment of open cities such as
occurred in World War II must be condemned).

There is also division regarding the second controversial limitation
on the means of warfare. All agree that in regard to megaton or upper-
level kiloton weapons "...it is not permissible to use them before the
other party has used them, or to take any advantage from their possession, except to deter other parties from using them." (para. 81) Some
would go further to say that "every power ought to make it clear that it
will not use the weapon even for purposes of retaliation." (para. 81)

The majority's preference of a cease-fire to all out war and the
prohibition of the first use of megaton weapons aroused considerable controversy. Anticipating this, the note added to introduce Chapter V[39]
singles them out for defense. In regard to para. 56 it is stated: "We
believe that an absolute limit must be set somewhere." (p. 29a) Non-
violent resistance is not a solution to all-out war nor does it guarantee
the preservation of freedom: "non violent resistance or non-resistance
may mean decades of tyranny and suffering" (p. 29a). The note also

---

[39] Ibid., pp. 29a-29b.

identifies two objections to the prohibition of the first use of megaton
weapons. To the idea that it unduly limits the freedom of military
action the note replies with the strategic argument that a limited
deterrent is more efficient because more certain than an unlimited
threat we would not dare to carry out. The objection from the other side
is that such a statement gives tacit consent to the use of smaller atomic
weapons; "...the answer would be that the proposal goes as far as there
is any hope of acceptance by the great powers now and that further steps
must follow if the envisaged discipline is to be realized" (p. 296). The
further goal is disarmament (para. 82), international control of states
(para. 57, 82), and ultimately the end of war (para. 85).

The same two points about cease-fire and the ban on first use were
controversial within the World Council of Churches bureaucracy,[40] and
certainly contributed[41] to the decision of the Central Committee to
entitle the report "A Provisional Study Document" and to place this
statement on the title page:

> The ensuing statement is but the first step in
> a continuing study process. It is offered to
> the Churches for their reflection and discussion.
> No point here expressed is to be understood as

---

[40] Ibid., cf. the accompanying notes, especially p. 38, and pp. 40-41.
There was even an attempt to restrict the reproduction of the document to
avoid misrepresentation of it, though the argument was not made clear
(pp. 42-43). The report of the central committee prior to the New Delhi
Assembly notes the document "caused vigorous debate in the Central Committee" and was both supported and criticized. However, it was decided
to offer the document to the churches for reflection and discussion and
it received much comment, particularly in Europe. Evanston to New Delhi:
1954-1961 (Geneva, 1961), p. 35.

[41] There were those on the other side of the issue who also requested
such a move. Martin Niemöller stated that making it official policy "would
bring those into great difficulty who do not believe that Christ would
allow his church under any circumstances to manufacture or use nuclear
weapons." Ibid., p. 43.

> an official view of the World Council of
> Churches. This document is in no sense a
> statement of World Council policy. Its
> standing is that of a contribution to
> Christian research and inquiry on a vital
> issue of our time.

Despite these difficulties the report did receive comment from
various quarters. For instance, faculty members from four theological
schools in the Eastern United States met over a period of time to study
the document and recommend changes. Some of them, joined by others,
produced a pamphlet entitled A Christian Approach to Nuclear War[42] which
I will use as a sample of nuclear pacifism. According to Christopher
Driver, "Even the U.S. State Department, it is said, was rather worried
by the World Council of Churches report...",[43] though he does not give
the source of that information.

In 1961, after receiving criticisms of the study, the officers of
the Commission published a revision of it.[44] The original paragraphs
66 (now 63) and 81 (now 75) which made the two controversial recommendations are substantially unchanged. What is new (para. 75) is increased
explicitness about the option that official plans not to resort to all
out war might be kept secret, and the idea that deemphasis on nuclear
weapons may require substantial increases in conventional forces.

---

[42] New York, n.d. Those listed as in essential agreement with it
are George Buttrick, Herbert Gezork, Walter Muelder, Arthur Cochrane,
Paul Deats, L. Harold De Wolf, Norman Gottwald, John Hick, Otto Piper,
and D. Campbell Wyckoff. Hereafter cited as Christian Approach.

[43] Christopher Driver, The Disarmers: A Study in Protest (London,
1964), p. 209.

[44] Thomas Taylor and Robert Bilheimer, Christians and the Prevention
of War in an Atomic Age (London, 1961).

Many of the issues brought out in Christians and the Prevention of War in an Atomic Age reverberate throughout the literature on modern war. I wish now only to call attention to four points: First of all, between 1948 and 1958 the position of "nuclear pacifism", not yet labeled, is beginning to emerge. Secondly, as in the Catholic teaching surveyed earlier, the emphasis is on the prevention of war, disarmament, and the establishment of international law and a world authority. Thirdly, there is little explicit reference here to the just war tradition, though some of its ideas, such as non-combatant immunity, are employed. In fact, the Taylor-Bilheimer edition rejects the just war concept because the present goal is to abolish, not justify, war, and because the concept of justice does not apply directly in the modern situation (para. 8). Finally, when it comes to making specific recommendations, and particularly those which limit the military actions which a government may threaten or perform, controversy is aroused. Perhaps this had something to do with the fact that, as far as I know, the promised "continuing study process" was never carried out by the World Council of Churches, at least not in reference to the work of this Commission.[45]

45
John Dayre complained that "The WCC authorities played [the original report] down as nothing more than a study document, which it did little to publicize." John Sayre, "The Church's Double Standard," Therefore Choose Life: Essays on the Nuclear Crisis (London, 1961), p. 31. However, the Executive Committee apparently did have at least some role in the publication of the Taylor-Bilheimer revision. Evanston to New Delhi: 1954-1961 (Geneva, 1961), p. 35. Also, the study did lead to a consultation between pacifists and non-pacifists, partly on the basis that "the development of atomic weapons has tended to cloud the pacifist/non-pacifist issue". Third Assembly of the World Council of Churches, "Report of the Committee on the Division of Studies," The New Delhi Report (New York, 1961), pp. 69-70. The book will be here-after cited as New Delhi Report.

The issue of nuclear weapons could not be and was not ignored, however. Apparently the idea of surrendering in certain circumstances was never again advocated, but the prohibition of first use of nuclear weapons was gradually accepted. A move in this direction was taken by the Third Assembly in New Delhi in 1961: "Christians must press most urgently upon their governments as a first step towards the elimination of nuclear weapons, never to get themselves into a position in which they contemplate the first use of nuclear weapons."[46] Moral concern is here cast in terms of politico-military advice, unlike the absolute statement which follows: "Christians must also maintain that the use of nuclear weapons, or other forms of major violence, against centres of population is in no circumstances reconcilable with the demands of the Christian Gospel."[47] Earlier in the same paragraph the report states: "The use of indiscriminate weapons must now be condemned by the churches as an affront to the Creator and a denial of the very purposes of the Creation."[48] No distinction is made between indiscriminate weapons and the indiscriminate use of weapons. It is also interesting to note that while the prohibition in either use involves the principle of discrimination, the statements are rooted directly in the Scriptural themes of creation and redemption rather than in the just war tradition or natural law. This perhaps reflects a Protestant tendency to prefer to reason explicitly from

---

[46] New Delhi Report, Report of the Section on Service, p. 108.
[47] Ibid.
[48] Ibid.

Scripture rather than from tradition, as well as the fact that Protestants have not developed just war casuistry as highly as Roman Catholics.

The report of the Fourth Assembly of the World Council of Churches did not discuss particular uses of nuclear weapons but it expressed general horror of nuclear war, not only because it would be suicidally destructive but because it would inflict lasting genetic damage. Thus,

> The churches must insist that it is the first
> duty of governments to prevent such a war: to
> halt the present arms race, agree never to
> initiate the use of nuclear weapons, stop exper-
> iments concerned with, and the production of
> weapons of mass human destruction by chemical
> and biological means and move away from the
> balance of terror towards disarmament.[49]

The verb "agree" makes it unclear whether or not the report is calling for, if necessary, a unilateral renunciation of the first use of nuclear weapons. In general the report does not specify actions that are uncon-ditionally prohibited but instead urges all nations to join in avoiding war and establishing peace and justice; this entails the establishment of a new world order, particularly through the strengthening of the United Nations.

There is no specific discussion in the Fourth Assembly of the morality of nuclear deterrence, only the exhortation to general disarmament. In fact, the report seems to give some (temporary) credence to the MAD deterrence policy by urging th U.S.A. and U.S.S.R. to agree not to develop anti-ballistic missile systems.[50] There were attempts both

---

[49]Fourth Assembly of the World Council of Churches, "Toward Justice and Peace in International Affairs," The Uppsala Report 1968 (Geneva, 1968), para. 11, p. 62. The book will be hereafter cited as Uppsala Report.

[50]Ibid., para. 12, p. 62.

within the section which prepared the report[51] and on the floor of the
assembly[52] to change the report to say that Christians can never be involved in preparing or threatening to use nuclear or other mass destruction weapons, but both attempts failed. However, there was support in
the text for pacifist conscientious objectors and selective conscientious
objectors, particularly in light of immoral means that may be used in
a particular war.[53]

There are many points of similarity between the statements of Rome
and statements of the World Council of Churches which I have surveyed.
First there is a general horror of modern war, particularly nuclear war,
with its potential for vast, indiscriminate, and long-lasting destruction.
Thus there is a new situation in which the right of nations to engage in
warfare must be greatly curtailed. Instead both Rome and the World
Council urge the building of international trust and cooperation on the
basis of justice secured by multilateral agreement, international law,
and the establishment of world authority, especially by the strengthening
of the United Nations. Along with this there must be general disarmament.
Since the goal is to abolish war, there is an attempt to transcend the
just war tradition, and in fact the World Council pays little attention
to it. Nevertheless some terms from that tradition are used, especially
discrimination or non-combatant immunity. Nuclear pacifism is emerging
but remains a minority position. However, there is more respect by the

---

[51] Uppsala Report, Paul Oestreicher, "Personal Comment on the Work of
the Section on Towards Justice and Peace in International Affairs," pp.
71-72.

[52] Uppsala Report, "Discussion of the Report on Towards Justice and
Peace in International Affairs," pp. 59-60.

[53] Uppsala Report, para. 21, p. 64.

majority for pacifism and conscientious objection. Unlike the World Council reports, Rome has begun to notice deterrence as a unique moral problem aside from any question of the use of nuclear weapons. In all of this there is a tone of general exhortation that we should expect in documents having an international perspective. Detailed application of these principles and goals is left to others.

A Definition of Nuclear Pacifism

We have now surveyed some of the main points in the development of
nuclear weapons and the strategic doctrines and debates concerning them,
as well as some of the statements of recent Popes, the Second Vatican
Council, and the World Council of Churches. I have not attempted to
describe international and national political developments such as crises
in Berlin and Cuba, the Campaign for Nuclear Disarmament in Britain, or
the passionate debate about fallout shelters in the United States,
through all of these were significant in the early 1960's when the
debate about nuclear weapons reached its peak. Instead I will rely on
the general knowledge of the reader in order to move on to a fuller
definition of the type of "nuclear pacifism" I am concerned with in
this study. My approach will be to make a series of increasingly
narrow distinctions between different views on the morality of war so
that, as it were, we can draw smaller and smaller concentric circles
until only nuclear pacifism is left in the center.

1) First of all, we must distinguish those who believe that warfare is subject to moral evaluation from those who do not. The latter
may simply be "cynics" or they may be "realists" who hold that a state
has its own "national interest" or "raison d'état" which it must pursue.
The nation itself then becomes the highest norm by which war may be
judged, not some (other) moral commitment.

2) There are those who do not hold the nation as such to be the
highest moral or theological/philosophical value but who view the nation
as the bearer of the highest value or values, such as Christianity, freedom, democracy, or civilization. The nation may then be called upon to

defeat other nations bearing other values, at least when challenged by
them. By historical analogy this may be called the "crusade" mentality.
In the present context it includes those who cry "Better dead than Red".
Opposing this view are those who believe that moral and theological/
philosophical values may be in conflict with the goals of the nation.

3) We are left with those who believe that warfare is subject to
moral evaluation by a standard that is (at least partially) independent
of the nation. Among these some are pacifists who claim that warfare is
always wrong, while others believe that it may sometimes be justified.
My concern is with the latter.

4) Among those remaining in this "circle" I would distinguish
between those who argue on the basis of general human prudence and those
who bring other moral commitments to bear on the problems of war. This
is not a clean distinction because the language of prudence probably
cannot be employed without moral terms and prudence is part of all moral
languages. My purpose here is to note that there are nuclear pacifists
who believe that it is simply foolish to employ nuclear weapons[54]
(including those who would say, "Better Red than dead") while there are
many others who believe that it would be simply foolish to get rid of
them unilaterally. My interest is in those who develop other types of

---

[54] E.g., Philip Toynbee, "Thoughts on Nuclear Warfare and a Policy to
Avoid It," The Fearful Choice: A Debate on Nuclear Policy (Detroit,
1959), pp. 9-22; Bertrand Russell, Common Sense and Nuclear Warfare (New
York, 1959); Stephen King-Hall, Defence in the Nuclear Age (Nyack, N.Y.,
1958) and Common Sense in Defense (London, 1960). It would be more
accurate to say that some nuclear pacifists use a kind of moral language other than the kind of moral language I am interested in. For
instance, Russell assumes the coincidence of common sense and morality,
while King-Hall talks of defending freedom and the democratic way of
life based on truth.

moral argument as well.

5) Furthermore, my concern is with those who argue on the basis of the Western just war tradition (cf. number 6 below) rather than on some other basis such as the Talmud, Marxist philosophy, or (only) the Christian New Testament.

6) Both Christians and non-Christians may in some way employ the Western just war tradition, but for the purposes of this study I am concerned with Christian thinkers. Most Catholics who argue in this vein are aware of a historical development, especially among Christians and, later, Roman Catholics, culminating in a more or less clearly defined set of principles. Some Protestant writers are much more vague about this history and have a much less defined language with which to evaluate warfare. In general I will consider those Christian writers who at least employ the criteria of discrimination and proportionality and who are willing to use them in some degree of casuistry as arguing from the just war tradition. Excluded are those who would propose a major alteration in the criteria[55] or who eschew casuistry.[56]

7) We are now left with Christian authors who maintain the continued validity of the Western just war tradition by using the just war criteria, at least non-combatant community and proportionality, in the

---

[55]E.g. William O'Brien would relativize the absolute character of the principle of non-combatant immunity. *Peace, Churches, Bomb*, p. 98; *Nuclear War, Deterrence and Morality* (New York, 1967), pp. 82-86.

[56]E.g. Angus Dun and Reinhold Niebuhr note the value of the traditional definition of a just war "as one in which just means are used to defend a just cause...But efforts to construct a precise guide through detailed elaborations of this definition result in a rigid and highly artificial structure, more likely to confuse than illumine the conscience." "God Wills Both Peace and Justice," *Christianity and Crisis*, XV (1955), 77.

analysis of modern warfare. Among these I would distinguish those who believe that nuclear weapons may sometimes be morally used and those who do not. There is no established term for the former but I will call them "counterforce theorists" or the like because they believe that the legitimate use of nuclear weapons on military targets may be possible. Among this group are: the American Protestant theological ethicist Paul Ramsey; the prominent American Roman Catholic theologian Fr. John Courtney Murray, S.J.; the British Catholic theologian Fr. Lawrence L. McReavy; the British Catholic theologian Fr. Paul Crane, S.J.; and the American Protestant social ethicist Theodore R. Weber. While I will in the following chapters cite other authors who could no doubt be described in this way, these five will serve as my principal representatives of the counterforce position.

8) Among those who believe that the actual use of nuclear weapons would be immoral there is disagreement about whether the threatened use of them (whether explicit or implicit) for the sake of deterrence would be immoral. At one point Paul Ramsey argues that it would not, and I will use his statement on the matter. A current advocate of this position is J. Bryan Hehir, the Associate Secretary for International Justice and Peace at the United States Catholic Conference. I will call this the "bluff" position because the term has been frequently used in ethical literature on the subject, and as far as I know the advocates of the position do not resent the term. It should be noted however that to my knowledge the term is not used in strategic debates.[57] When those

---

[57] Pierce Corden, a Physical Science Officer of the U.S. Arms Control and Disarmament Agency, advocates the position but does not use the term. Pierce Corden, "Ethics and Deterrence: Moving Beyond the Just-War Traditions," Ford and Winters, ENS?, pp. 156-180.

who hold the bluff position are excluded, only nuclear pacifists of a
certain type (Christians who employ the Western just war tradition)
remain in our final "circle". In fact I will draw the circle even smaller
to include only writers from the English-speaking lands, for it will be
difficult enough to do justice to them without expanding the project
further. An advantage of this limitation is that there is a great deal
of interaction between many of the authors I will discuss.

No typology, especially one as sweeping as that given above, can
claim to draw sharp lines of distinction between the many views on a
subject as complex as modern war. Nevertheless it has brought us to a
position from which I can now offer a general definition of nuclear
pacifism (in its generic sense, see below). Based on the logic of the
position and my observation of the actual usage of the term, "nuclear
pacifism" includes these points: 1) The affirmation that theoretically,
at least in the past, a given war might be justified. 2) The judgment
that any (large-scale) use of a certain class of weapons is immoral.
3) The judgment that any threatened use of such weapons, even in self-
defense or retaliation, is immoral. 4) The claim that these moral
judgments require unconditioned action, including if necessary the unilateral disarmament of nuclear or other weapons by one's own government.

Some things should be noted about this definition. First, point 1
is necessary to distinguish it from absolute or traditional pacifism.
Secondly, item 2 places "large-scale" in parenthesis because nuclear
pacifists may admit that a given use of an individual weapon could be
licit but they deny that this removes that class of weapons from censure.
Thirdly, the type of weapons or warfare proscribed must at least poten-

tially be militarily very important; condemnation of a relatively unimportant weapon does not make one a nuclear pacifist. Fourthly, although the distinction between tactical and strategic or atomic and hydrogen nuclear weapons may be important, I will consider nuclear pacifism to require the repudiation of all nuclear weapons, not only strategic or hydrogen ones. Fifthly, statement 3 distinguishes nuclear pacifism from the bluff position. I believe that this reflects general usage, even though J. Bryan Hehir considers himself to be a type of nuclear pacifist.[58] Finally, in regard to point 4 nuclear pacifists advocate unilateral action if multilateral action cannot be quickly accomplished. However, Justus George Lawler, who considers himself a nuclear pacifist,[59] does not advocate unilateral nuclear disarmament. Nevertheless if the word "pacifism" in the term is to receive its proper weight, unconditional commitment must be implied. Thus unilateralism is included in the definition in order to distinguish nuclear pacifists from those who put their hopes entirely in multilateral disarmament and from those who simply condemn modern war without specifying what immediate moral demands this implies.

The cases of Hehir and Lawler cited above make it clear that there is no universally agreed upon definition of "nuclear pacifism", although I believe that my definition fits most usage. Even my definition will

---

[58] J. Bryan Hehir, "The Just-War Ethic and Catholic Theology: Dynamics of Change and Continuity," War or Peace? The Search for New Answers ed. Thomas Shannon (Maryknoll, N.Y., 1980), pp. 27-28. However, in the same article (p. 29) Hehir does assume, as I do, that nuclear pacifism requires the condemnation of the use of all nuclear weapons, not just strategic ones.

[59] Justus George Lawler, "Moral Issues and Nuclear Pacifism," Peace, Churches, Bomb, p. 94.

leave some doubtful cases of classification, which is probably inevitable
in view of the complexity of the subject and the fact that authors do not
always answer all the questions we might ask of them. Most of the authors
I have selected as samples of nuclear pacifism for this study do fall
clearly within the definition I have given. The earliest is Fr. John
Kenneth Ryan, an American Catholic philosopher, who already in 1933 seemed
to conclude that no modern war could pass the scrutiny of the just war
criteria.[60] In September, 1944 the American Catholic moral theologian
Fr. John C. Ford, S.J., published an important article in which he
criticized the "obliteration bombing" then being conducted on German
industrial cities by British and American forces.[61] He later argued
that any hydrogen bombing of cities would likewise be immoral.[62] In
1959 there appeared a little book entitled Morals and Missiles: Catholic
Essays on the Problems of War Today.[63] Its contributors were English
Catholic churchmen and others and it exhibited a great deal of nuclear

---

[60] John K. Ryan, "Modern War and Basic Ethics," (Unpublished doctoral
dissertation, Catholic University of America, 1933). Hereafter cited as
Ryan, "Modern War." It was published in 1940 (Milwaukee) under the same
title. However, Ryan later supported America's position in World War
II and denied that his work ruled out all modern war. John K. Ryan, "The
Catholic Conscientious Objector and Some Traditional Principles,"
Ecclesiastical Review, CVIII (1943), 348-356.

[61] John C. Ford, "The Morality of Obliteration Bombing," Theological
Studies, V (1944), 261-309. Hereafter cited as Ford, "Obliteration Bombing". Ford cited Ryan and believed that his book in itself ruled out the
possibility of any just modern war. Ford, "Obliteration Bombing,"
pp. 291-292.

[62] John C. Ford, "The Hydrogen Bombing of Cities," Theology Digest,
V (1957), 6-9.

[63] Charles S. Thompson, ed., Morals and Missiles: Catholic Essays
on the Problem of War Today (London, 1959). Hereafter cited as Morals
and Missiles.

pacifism. The essay by E. I. Watkin entitled "Unjustifiable War"[64] is a clear, terse statement of nuclear pacifism and one of the most well-known representatives of it. Undoubtedly the high-water mark of nuclear pacifism as I have defined it was reached with the publication in 1961 of the book entitled Nuclear Weapons and the Christian Conscience.[65] It contained essays by British Catholic lay writers including the philosophers Elizabeth Anscombe, R. A. Markus, and Peter Geach; an unidentified Roger Smith; and Walter Stein, a lecturer in philosophy and English literature. Stein also edited and contributed to a follow-up book entitled Peace on Earth,[66] which was designed to offer more specific proposals for achieving justice, peace, disarmament and non-violent resistance.

Moving back to the United States and this time to Protestants, the theologian Norman K. Gottwald advocated nuclear pacifism in the early 1960's.[67] He was also involved with others in distributing the nuclear pacifist document A Christian Approach to Nuclear War, which I have mentioned previously. The Protestant theologian Donald Bloesch also espoused nuclear pacifism, though in many respects he argued very diff-

---

[64] E. I. Watkin, "Unjustifiable War," Morals and Missiles, pp. 51-62. Hereafter cited as Watkin, "Unjustifiable War."

[65] Walter Stein, ed., Nuclear Weapons and Christian Conscience (London, 1961). Hereafter cited as Stein, NWCC.

[66] Walter Stein, ed., Peace on Earth: The Way Ahead (London, 1966). Hereafter cited as Stein, Peace on Earth.

[67] Norman K. Gottwald, "Nuclear Realism or Nuclear Pacifism?," Christian Century, LXXVII (1960), 895-899, hereafter cited as Gottwald, "NR or NP?"; "Moral and Strategic Reflections on the Nuclear Dilemma," Christianity and Crisis, XXI (1962), 239-242, hereafter cited as Gottwald, "Reflections."

erently than other nuclear pacifists, since his approach was based more on Reinhold Niebuhr than on the just war criteria.[68] Finally, the only more recent nuclear pacifist in our sample is the American Catholic Fr. Francis X. Winters, S.J., who is an associate professor of moral theology at Georgetown University's School of Foreign Service. He also lectures at the Army War College. Winters contributed to and co-edited the symposium entitled Ethics and Nuclear Strategy?, which I have cited previously. Occasionally I will also cite other nuclear pacifists in order to make a certain point.

It might be questioned whether a few of these authors are nuclear pacifists as I have defined them. For instance, neither Ford nor Anscombe specify whether they would object to all use of nuclear weapons or only the countervalue use of them.[69] During World War II Ford did not believe that nuclear war was necessarily total, but he declared that if it were shown to be so, it must be rejected: "So much the worse for modern war."[70] The fact that his second article

---

[68]Donald Bloesch, "The Christian and the Drift Towards War," Theology and Life, II (1959), 318-326.

[69]Paul Ramsey discusses the Ford article "Obliteration Bombing" approvingly in his first book, in which he was most critical of nuclear weapons. Paul Ramsey, War and the Christian Conscience: How Shall Modern War Be Conducted Justly? (Durham, North Carolina, 1961), pp. 70-83. However, Ramsey in the same book (p. 76) finds Ford's assumption in "The Hydrogen Bombing of Cities," op. cit., p. 8, that war with hydrogen bombs would probably end civilization a bit too sweeping. Elizabeth Anscombe's article is entitled "War and Murder" and is found in Stein, NWCC, pp. 45-62. Hereafter cited as Anscombe, "War and Murder ". Ramsey does not discuss it except to adopt its criticism of pacifism. Ramsey, Just War, p. 297.

[70]Ford, "Obliteration Bombing," pp. 267-268.

dealt only with hydrogen bombs could imply that he would not make the same claim about atomic bombs, but this is not certain. At any rate, these questions must be borne in mind when I cite Fr. Ford.

In "War and Murder" Elizabeth Anscombe condemns the "obliteration bombing of cities" but does not specifically mention nuclear weapons. She cites examples of the just employment of conventional weapons by smaller powers (p. 60), but she assumes that it is "unimaginable" that a major war between the Great Powers would not be "a set of enormous massacres of civil populations" (p. 59). Also she condemns any preparation for a "war with Russia involving the deliberate massacre of cities" (p. 62), even if it means risking Russian domination. Thus Anscombe implicitly seems to equate nuclear weapons with the massacre of cities. This, plus the fact that her essay was published in a clearly nuclear pacifist book, make it a reasonable presumption that Anscombe fits our definition of a nuclear pacifist. Donald Bloesch also does not explicitly call for national unilateral nuclear disarmament, but this is probably due to pessimism about whether the state would adopt such a course.

The fact that Ryan and Ford in my sample both wrote pieces prior to the invention of the atom bomb suggests that there are disadvantages in the term "nuclear pacifism". Various expressions have been used to describe the view that while some wars in the past might have been justified, modern war or some types of it cannot be: "modern pacifism";[71]

---

[71] Christopher Hollis, "The Two Pacifisms," Morals and Missiles, pp. 47-50.

"relative Christian pacifism";[72] "neo-pacifism";[73] "practical pacifism";[74] "unilateralism";[75] "just war pacifism".[76] The expression "nuclear pacifism" has been used in English at least since 1960 with the publication of Norman Gottwald's article "Nuclear Realism or Nuclear Pacifism?". In view of the destructiveness and military/political significance of nuclear weapons, it is not surprising that they have influenced the choice of expression which came to represent the position.

Nevertheless "nuclear pacifism" is not an adequate generic term because other types of indiscriminate or disproportionate weapons may be condemned, such as chemical or bacteriological weapons. During World War II Vera Brittain not only criticized obliteration bombing but called for agreement to ban the use of the bombing aeroplane once peace returned.[77] Some believe that because of the risk of the escalation of conflict no war can be justified in the nuclear age; others may simply conclude that following unilateral disarmament it would be futile to try to oppose a nuclear enemy with any kind of violent resistance. Thus ideally "modern-war pacifism" might be a better generic term to cover all of these cases, and "nuclear pacifism" reserved to describe those who condemn only nuc-

---

[72] John Courtney Murray, Morality and Modern War (New York, 1959). Hereafter cited as Murray, MMW.

[73] Ernest W. Lefever, "The Ethics of Calculation," Worldview, II (1959), 6-8; reprinted as "Facts, Calculation and Political Ethics" in The Moral Dilemma of Nuclear Weapons (New York, 1961), pp. 38-43.

[74] L. L. McReavy, Peace and War in Catholic Doctrine (Oxford, 1963), pp. 13-14. Hereafter cited as McReavy, Peace.

[75] Stein, Peace on Earth.

[76] Theodore Weber, Modern War and the Pursuit of Peace (New York, 1968). Hereafter cited as Weber, MWPP.

[77] Vera Brittain, Seed of Chaos: What Mass Bombing Really Means (London, 1944), p. 117.

lear weapons.[78] However, because nuclear weapons do receive by far the
most attention, and because the differences noted above are often only
a matter of emphasis rather than of dispute, I will follow popular usage
and employ "nuclear pacifism" as a generic term. When distinctions are
needed they will be made clear from the context.

---

[78] James T.Johnson does this when he says that nuclear pacifism is
the most common form of modern-war pacifism. "Just War Theory: What's
the Use?," Worldview, XIX (1976), p. 43. However, Johnson does not
describe other types of modern-war pacifism. At the same time we
should note that use of the term "modern-war pacifism" could itself be
confusing. It could be used not only as a generic but also as a
specific term to indicate the conviction that all modern war is wrong.

The Plan of This Study

Since I have now defined the type of nuclear pacificm which is the subject of this study I can outline my plan for the rest of the work. I hope to accomplish three things. The first is to provide a full description of this type of nuclear pacifism so that its logic, judgments, and variations are clear. That can only be adequately done by locating it in the general debate about modern warfare. I will be particularly interested in contrasting it with the counterforce position, since the two views both claim to represent the just war tradition. At a couple of points I will also contrast nuclear pacifism with the bluff position, which also employs just war thought to ban the actual use of nuclear weapons.

On the basis of my descriptive account I will be able to attempt my second goal which is to offer some criticisms of nuclear pacifism, the counterforce theory, and the bluff position. Thirdly, I will ask what the whole debate shows about the status of the just war tradition itself in the nuclear age.

Since this dissertation concerns the moral "position" of nuclear pacifism it would not be sufficient to present the ideas of one or two authors. Therefore I have selected for study the individuals mentioned above because they are important in the development of nuclear pacifism or because they explicitly argue for it. I will make the most use of Walter Stein, who has probably argued the case for nuclear pacifism more extensively than anyone else, and who is often considered its chief exponent, but I will frequently cite other authors as well.

In the descriptive portion of the dissertation, chapters two through five, I will organize the material according to a structure which I

believe to cover the main issues with which nuclear pacifism deals.
Where feasible I will use categories employed by my sources themselves,
without attempting to evaluate the adequacy of those categories.
Throughout I will present the material in the form of a dialogue between
nuclear pacifists and their critics. Often I will not try to locate
critics in any particular "circle" of my typology above. However, at
times I will specify a counterforce or bluff argument, and Ramsey, Weber,
Crane, McReavy and John Courtney Murray can always be assumed to represent
the counterforce position. I will use Paul Ramsey as the main spokes-
person for the counterforce position, because he has argued it most
extensively and because of his prominence in the field.

Usually theologians and philosophers will be my main sources rather
than ecclesiastic statements (except for some from the American Roman
Catholic bishops) or more popular writings, both of which tend to be
less technical and explicit in their moral argumentation. Limited
attention will be given to works from the fields of strategic analysis,
political science, and so forth. Most of my important sources date
between 1959 and 1966, simply because that was the heyday of nuclear
pacifism and of the general discussion about the morality of nuclear
weapons.

The nuclear pacifist position holds together like a spider web,
though it may not be as strong and symmetrical. As I lead the reader in
an attempt to trace its patterns we are confronted by two dangers. If we
try to strictly isolate one strand of argument at a time, we can only do
so by pulling it away from the web entirely, thus destroying the fabric
of the position. On the other hand, if at every intersection we try to

explore each new line of thought, we shall quickly become bewildered and probably end up kicking and thrashing, hopelessly entangled in the sticky strands of the web. Therefore our best strategy is to follow one strand at a time, observe each intersection as we come to it, and proceed with caution. My only promise is that if the reader has enough patience, we will eventually explore the whole web.

With that strategy in mind I can now briefly map out our itinerary. I will conclude this chapter with a few remarks on the factors involved in ethical debate. In Chapter Two I will show why nuclear pacifists believe--and their critics dispute--that on the basis of the just war criteria it cannot be just to fight a modern war, at least not with nuclear weapons. Chapter Three deals with the issue of whether or not it is licit to attempt to deter war using nuclear weapons. Since nuclear pacifists conclude that it is immoral to fight or deter with nuclear weapons, they believe it is only logical to demand of their governments nuclear disarmament, even if it must be unilateral. In Chapter Four I will describe the debate about the consequences of this and alternative policies, especially in view of the East/West conflict, and the methodological question that this raises about the role of consequentialist reasoning in ethics. This discussion in turn points out the necessity of hope, which makes radical obedience possible, and I begin Chapter Five with that topic. Since hope would seem to be based on a particular commitment, the issue is raised about whether the just war ethic is universal or particular in scope. Along with this Christian nuclear pacifists and critics must define what they believe to be the role of the church in facing the ethical issues of nuclear weapons. Finally, in Chapter Six I will offer my own criticisms of nuclear pacifism, the counterforce moral theory, and the bluff position. Then I will demonstrate that the nuclear age has raised some new and fundamental challenges to the just war tradition itself.

Factors Involved in Ethical Debate

Up to this point I have set the stage for a more detailed discussion of nuclear pacifism and some of the other views with which it contends. Before describing that debate, however, it would be well to take note of some of the many factors that enter into any discussion of ethical decisions.[79] First of all, every debate requires communication and thus a community sharing a common language. Since we all belong to any number of communities at the same time, it is important to observe what language is being used and what community is being urged to act. Secondly, appeal is generally made to a particular moral tradition, which upholds certain authorities, norms, values, dispositions, and so forth. Depending upon how broadly "community" and "tradition" are defined, a given community may carry different moral traditions, and/or different communities may bear the same tradition. Thirdly, it is necessary in any ethical discussion to assess what "empirical" data is relevant to the issue at hand and what the actual "facts" are. Fourthly, there are different types of ethical reasoning, such as teleology, deontology, intuition, and that based upon character. Finally, there are broad philosophical/theological assumptions, such as those concerning the nature of man, divine providence, and so forth, upon which there may be agreement or disagreement.

Occasionally in an ethical debate, disagreement may be located exclusively in one of these factors. For instance, two authors might

---

[79] Ralph Potter borrows from Talcott Parsons to develop extensive but somewhat different paradigms of these factors in "The Structure of Certain American Christian Responses to the Nuclear Dilemma, 1958-1963," (Unpublished doctoral dissertation, Harvard University, 1965). For a condensed version see Ralph Potter, War and Moral Discourse (Richmond, Virginia, 1969), pp. 23-24.

disagree about the purely factual matter of how many megaton warheads a country possesses. More often, a disagreement about a certain issue involves several of these factors at once. For instance, the question of whether nuclear war could remain "limited" depends upon whether or not the disputants are using the same language when they both speak of "limited war", upon factual assumptions about command and control procedures governing the use of nuclear weapons, upon anthropological convictions about the rationality of people, and so forth. Parties in a debate may not be aware that all of these elements are involved in a difference on opinion.

Because of these interconnections I have judged it more fruitful to structure the dissertation around particular issues than around the various factors in the debate. It would be well to bear in mind, however, that any or all of them may be involved in any particular point or counterpoint that these authors make.

Chapter II

MODERN WAR AND THE JUST WAR CRITERIA

An Old Tradition in a New Situation

By definition, the nuclear pacifists with whom we are concerned in
this study affirm at least the theoretical validity of the just war
tradition. Even if they do not mention this tradition by name they affirm
it by arguing at least in part on the basis of its criteria. Even if
their critics sometimes lump them together, "nuclear pacifists" are not
pacifists who deny that it is ever right to kill. What makes these
writers "nuclear pacifists" is the conviction that while the principles
of the just war tradition remains valid, the nature of war has changed so
drastically that the old principles require new conclusions. Norman
Gottwald states it pointedly when he says that: "Everywhere men are
awakening to the fact that ours is the first generation in an utterly
new era."[1]

In summarizing the view of the contributors to Nuclear Weapons and
Christian Conscience, Walter Stein alludes to both the traditional perspective and the new situation:

> We are not saying that war can never, in
> principle, be justified. Nor that there
> are not powerful motives in justice--and
> even charity--to protect our countries against
> communist aggression. We can envisage

---

[1] Gottwald, "NR or NP?" p. 895.

> situations in which, other things being equal,
> we _ought_ to defend our countries--our liberty,
> our institutions--by force, even at enormous
> sacrifice. The point is that other things are
> not equal: their name is "massive nuclear bom-
> bardment" and "virtual annihilation."[2]

Because of the new military developments, Stein and other nuclear

pacifists are no longer content to judge only the validity of particular

military actions and particular wars as was usually done in the past.

Instead they use the just war criteria to judge whole weapons systems

and forms of modern warfare. In this chapter I will discuss only the

issue of the validity of fighting modern war; in the next chapter I will

discuss the related issue of what may be done in deterring war.

---

[2]Stein, _NWCC_, p. 30. The terms quoted are from a British White
Paper and President Eisenhower, respectively, both in 1958.

The Criterion of Discrimination

The two most important criteria in the debate about nuclear pacifism are those of discrimination and proportionality. The principle of discrimination belongs to the category of just means in warfare. It states that only guilty persons, that is, enemy combatants, are subject to direct attack in warfare. Thus the principle is sometimes called "non-combatant immunity" or the "immunity of the innocent." According to just war theorists, only direct killing of the innocent, even in a just war, is to be classified as murder.

The principle of discrimination does not mean that under no circumstances may innocent persons be killed. Noncombatants may be killed as long as their death is unavoidable and incidental to an attack against a military target. Such killing is "indirect" and may be justified by the "principle of double effect." In Catholic moral thought the principle of double effect serves to justify certain actions which seem prima facie wrong without granting that "the end justifies the means." An action which has both a good and a bad effect may be done without incurring moral guilt if it meets four criteria: 1) The act itself must be morally good or indifferent; i.e. certain inherently evil actions cannot be justified by this principle. 2) The agent must intend only the good, not the evil, effect of the act. 3) Both effects must be the immediate result of the action; i.e. the evil effect cannot be the means to the good effect. 4) The good effect must be proportionate to the evil effect.[3]

_____

[3]Michael Duffey, "A Study of the Principle of Double Effect," (Unpublished doctoral dissertation, University of Notre Dame, 1981), pp. v-vii; Joseph McKenna, "Ethics and War: A Catholic View," American Political Science Review, LIV (1960), 647-658.

According to the nuclear pacifists, the killing of noncombatants is central and not incidental to modern war. Fr. John K. Ryan stated in 1933 that attack on civilian populations, which was already evident in the American Civil War and the Franco-Prussian War, was carried further with the use of gas and aerial bombardment in the First World War: "The air weapon, gas and flame are essentially offensive weapons, adapted by nature to attacks on large, densely populated, undefended and indefensible areas." He concluded that while attacks on civilians were not essential to past wars, "modern total war will be marked by sudden and, if possible, completely devastating attacks upon the non-combatant civil population."[4]

Unfortunately, Fr. Ryan's words proved prophetic, and complete devastation was proven possible, in the course of World War II. In 1944 John C. Ford, S.J., published an article in Theological Studies entitled "The Morality of Obliteration Bombing" in which he condemned the bombing of German and other cities then being conducted by the British and American forces.[5] With the development and use of the atomic bomb, the development of the hydrogen bomb, and the formulation of the policy of massive retaliation, it seemed obvious to some moralists that nuclear war inherently meant the abrogation of the principle of discrimination. As E.I. Watkin says: "Right means alone will not be used in any such major war. For on both sides weapons are being perfected and accumulated which

---

[4]John K. Ryan, "Modern War and Basic Ethics," (Doctoral dissertation, Catholic University of America, 1933), pp. 85-87, quotations from p. 87. Hereafter cited as Ryan, "Modern War".

[5]John C. Ford, "The Morality of Obliteration Bombing," Theological Studies, V (1944), 261-309. Hereafter cited as Ford, "Obliteration Bombing."

will massacre and mutilate millions of innocent non-combatants (whole cities can now be wiped out of existence)...".[6]

In view of the apparent conflict between fact and principle, nuclear pacifists choose to uphold principle. However, there are those who claim that the principle of discrimination is not relevant to the conditions of modern total war, in which all members of society contribute to the war effort. Therefore all members of an enemy society may be considered guilty and subject to direct attack. This view is not, as far as I know, held in such extreme form by any moralist. The one who comes closest is the British Catholic L.L. McReavy in an article published in March, 1941.[7] He supports the unanimous claim of just war theologians that the state may never directly intend to kill the innocent (133), but notes that today the difficult question is:

> ...who are the innocent, the harmless, the non-aggressive?...To decide that, we must ask who in fact contribute actively to the inception and maintenance of the aggression. And if the answer leads logically to the inclusion of munition-workers among the aggressors who may be directly attacked, where, we may ask, in this age of totalitarian warfare, when whole nations are harnessed to the common struggle and all, male and female, old and young, are expected to contribute their maximum effort, where are we to draw the line? (134)

Later McReavy concludes that: "The innocent--that is to say, the harmless (if, apart from infants, there are any)--are, of course, immune from direct attack on their lives; but in modern conditions the theologian

---

[6]Watkin, "Unjustifiable War," p. 52.

[7]L.L. McReavy, "Reprisals: A Second Opinion," Clergy Review, XX (1941), 131-138. Hereafter cited as McReavy, "Reprisals."

cannot tell who they are, and the attacking airman does not know where they are. (138, author's italics)

McReavy does not want this difficulty to undermine "the Christian mitigations of warfare" and permit a "reversion to barbarism" in the conclusion that a whole nation is a legitimate object of direct attack (134). Instead he proposes that only fighting forces and the factories which supply them may normally be attacked, because the degree of aggression of civilians is so small that it would be an inordinate amount of violence to seek to kill them. However, the property of enemy subjects is not absolutely immune. For instance, the British government has declared that the best response to German nighttime bombing is "to hammer the enemy's bases and factories."

> But suppose circumstances were to change, and it became clear that the only effective way of preventing Germany from reducing all our cities to rubble was to smash a few of theirs by way of reprisal, then it seems to me that the Government would be quite justified in ordering such action and our airmen in executing it. They must not directly intend the killing of the innocent, for that is intrinsically evil. But there is nothing intrinsically evil in the destruction of enemy civilian property... (137)

To what extent circumstances changed might be debated, but it is clear that a year or two later Sir Arthur Harris, head of the British Bomber Command, targeted eighty German cities for massive bombing. With this in mind, John C. Ford notes that, "Dr. McReavy is the only Catholic moralist I know of who makes the appalling insinuation that only infants are innocent in a modern war....I think it is an appalling insinuation because for all practical purposes it means discarding the distinction between innocent and guilty altogether...".[8] According to Ford the weaker restrictions that McReavy provides offer "no real safeguard against the savagery of total war."[9]

Nevertheless, Ford does have to admit that under the changed conditions of modern war it is not possible to draw according to natural law a precise line between combatants and non-combatants. But it is enough to show that many people still are innocent non-combatants and that their rights are violated by obliteration bombing.[10] He uses lists and figures to demonstrate that in a modern industrial country at least three-quarters of the total civilian population are non-combatants.[11] At the same time, Ford notes that the change in the conditions of war must not be exaggerated:

> Armies in the past had to be supplied with food,
> clothing, guns, and ammunition, and it was the
> civilian population who supplied them. The Church
> and the theologians in declaring civilians innocent
> realized very well that even in former times

---

[8]Ford, "Obliteration Bombing," p. 276, note 41.

[9]Ibid. McReavy himself later altered his position to claim that "a very considerable portion" of the citizens of an aggressor state are innocent, "even if account be taken only of the children, the sick and the aged." However, he continued to maintain that the property of the innocent was not inviolable, and an evacuated town could be bombed. Cf. McReavy, Peace, pp. 33-36; quotations from p. 35.

[10]Ford, "Obliteration Bombing," pp. 280-281. Walter Stein makes a similar point: Stein, NWCC, p. 27.

[11]Ford, "Obliteration Bombing," pp. 283-286. Those whom Ford allows as questionable are workers involved in weapons production, mining, transportation, communications, and public offices close to the war, p. 285.

> civilian sympathies, their moral support, and
> their actual physical aid went to further the
> cause of their country.[12]

Nuclear pacifists face a challenge not only from those who disagree about the relevance of the principle of discrimination but from those who empathetically agree about its relevance. Counterforce advocates base their position precisely on this principle. Paul Ramsey, for instance, argues throughout his work that one central and unbreakable rule of war is that civilians are to be protected from direct attack: "countercity" military action is inherently immoral while "counterforces" attack is not. Thus Ramsey supports Ford in his criticism of McReavy[13] and joins nuclear pacifists in condemning the bombings of Dresden, Tokyo, Hiroshima and Nagasaki.[14] It is in regard to the application of the principle of discrimination that nuclear pacifists and counterforce theorists disagree. At this point our discussion will be directed to nuclear weapons, though the arguments would have some relevance to other weapons of mass destruction as well.

There are three arguments which counterforce just war moralists use to refute nuclear pacifism while maintaining the principle of noncom-

---

[12]Ibid., p. 283.

[13]Paul Ramsey, War and the Christian Conscience: How Shall Modern War Be Conducted Justly? (Durham, N.C., 1961), pp. 73-75. Hereafter cited as Ramsey, WCC.

[14]E.g. Ramsey, Just War, pp. 348, 353-355, 534.

batant immunity. The first is that there can be no blanket condemnation of nuclear weapons because in some cases their use can be confined to military targets. On the one hand, there are some very small tactical nuclear weapons which can be used like any other artillery shell, while on the other hand there are appropriate military targets even for larger weapons. Both points are made by Fr. Paul Crane, S.J., of England in reaction to E.I. Watkin's claim in Morals and Missiles[15] that, in Crane's words, "nuclear weapons of war are of such a nature that they are indiscriminate in their effects." He counters that:

> The terms of the argument are too sweeping. Its fault lies in its lack of qualification. Mr. Watkin would seem to assume that the use of nuclear weapons by a just defendant is necessarily to be identified with the direct massacre of the innocent through the indiscriminate hydrogen bombing of an unjust aggressor's cities and towns. It need not be, for there are now in existence controlled nuclear devices which can be restricted to military targets. At the same time, one can conceive of military targets on which a certain type of nuclear bomb could be used whilst remaining discriminate in its effects: such, for example, could be a fleet at sea.[16]

Walter Stein cites and then refutes this passage in a style that cannot be summarized:

> Such arguments are unanswerable. All one can do, perhaps, is to mention a few relevant considerations. One might, for instance, indicate that whilst "controlled nuclear devices" are no doubt

---

[15] Watkin, "Unjustifiable War," pp. 52-53; see above.

[16] Paul Crane, "Catholics and Nuclear War," The Month, XXII (1959), 223-229. Hereafter cited as Crane, "Catholics".

> very ingenious inventions, it is difficult to
> restrict governments to controlled nuclear
> devices. This, one might add, would seem all
> the more important where governments have in
> fact categorically proclaimed 'to any potential
> aggressor the prospect of virtual annihilation
> of his own country'. Then there is that 'fleet
> at sea' (it is remarkable how this fleet keeps
> turning up in this connexion): one has to admit,
> 'a certain type of nuclear bomb' <u>could</u> be used
> against it--and used with impressive efficiency--
> whilst remaining discriminate in its effects;
> though this still leaves the question how many
> of these fleets, or armies concentrating in
> deserts, perhaps, are likely to be about. What
> we do, on the other hand, know with some direct-
> ness is that many hundreds or thousands of 'a
> certain type of bomb'...are accumulating in
> various parts of the globe.[17]

For Stein and other nuclear pacifists the dominating image of a nuclear

explosion is the destruction of a city and the dominating image of

nuclear war is the destruction of civilization. It is thus irrelevant

if not dangerous to talk of those rare cases of the legitimate use of

nuclear weapons. Nevertheless the argument does point out that the con-

demnation of <u>all</u> nuclear weapons rests partially upon certain judgements

of fact that may be challenged, such as the limited number of legitimate

nuclear targets and the probability of any nuclear exchange leading to

full-scale nuclear war (see below). Thus Justus George Lawler personally

believes that any nuclear war would result in total war, but since this

cannot be "logically demonstrated" he urges the Second Vatican Council

to condemn only weapons with no military target, such as the Russian 100

megaton bomb, and superfluous stockpiles of nuclear weapons with no

---

[17]Stein, <u>NWCC</u>, pp. 34-35.

justifiable military target.[18]

The first argument which counterforce theorists use to avoid drawing nuclear pacifist conclusions from the principle of discrimination thus assumes that there are instances in which nuclear weapons may be used agasint military targets with little or no attendant or "collateral" harm to civilians (and their property). The second argument is that even extensive collateral harm may be justified by the principle of double effect (see above). The key issue is whether the collateral harm to civilians may be considered as directly intended or not. Elizabeth Anscombe attacks the "double-think about double effect" which would make intention merely an act of the will, so that any means can be justified as long as only the ultimate end is desired.[19] However, the principle is not employed in this way by serious moralists.[20]

More importantly, Catholic nuclear pacifists argue that the damage of nuclear warfare would be so great that it could not be considered

---

[18]Justus George Lawler, "Moral Issues and Nuclear Pacifism," Peace, the Churches and the Bomb (New York, 1965), p. 93. Hereafter cited as Peace, Churches, Bomb with the name of the individual author. Also Justus George Lawler, Nuclear War: the Ethic, the Rhetoric, the Reality (Westminster, Maryland, 1965), p. 63. Hereafter cited as Lawler, Nuclear War.

[19]G.E.M. Anscombe, "War and Murder," Nuclear Weapons and Christian Conscience, ed. Walter Stein (London, 1961), pp. 57-59. Hereafter cited as Anscombe, "War and Murder".

[20]Again, it is L.L. McReavy in the article discussed above (McReavy, "Reprisals") who comes the closest. Paul Ramsey interprets McReavy's acceptance of the bombing of civilian property in this way: "This seems to mean that a bombardier may let go the bombs at the munition worker's houses, and at the homes of their grocers, cobblers, barbers, etc. and at their lives, but withhold the intention so far as their lives are concerned." (Ramsey, WCC, p. 74, author's italics) He presumes, though, that the civilians would have been warned in advance.

"indirect." Sometimes this judgment is based on the expected results
of an all-out war of "massive retaliation,"[21] therefore failing to
meet the argument based on limited, counterforce nuclear warfare.
However, Justus George Lawler (whom we may here take as arguing the
nuclear pacifist position) does calculate that a full-scale (15,000
megaton) but strictly counterforce American attack "would kill almost
all of the people of Russia. Obviously we have gone beyond any calculation of double effect."[22] Nothing within the scope of man's
imagination would render just such devastation and murder. In the discussion which follows Ramsey takes Lawler to task for calling such an
action "murder." According to Ramsey only violation of the principle
of discrimination may be called "murder," and Lawler's judgment is
based on the principle of proportionality, which is not involved in the
rule of double effect. Confusion arises here because when Lawler considers war a single act, the criterion of proportionality within the
principle of double effect becomes coextensive with the just war criterion
of proportionality. The issue becomes important in evaluating deterrence
policies and I will discuss it further in Chapter 5. For now I will
simply note that according to Ramsey, as long as one does not enlarge
a target and the target itself is important enough to justify the collateral damage which will inevitably attend its destruction, such collateral

---

[21]E.g., Stein, NWCC, pp. 28-29.

[22]Justus George Lawler, Peace, Churches, Bomb, p. 35. The discussion
is continued on pp. 54 (Ramsey), 88 (Lawler), and 99 (O'Brien), and in
Ramsey, Just War, pp. 347-356. The figures might themselves be disputed.
As I interpret the figures provided by Fred Kaplan in Dubious Specter
(Washington, D.C., 1980), p. 88, U.S. strategic weapons in January, 1980,
totaled less than 3,500 megatons. However, in the discussion the figures
themselves were not disputed.

damage is indirect and unintended according to the principle of double effect.[23]

L.L. McReavy is one counterforce theorist who does affirm that a weighing of good and evil consequences is part of the principle of double effect, and he is willing to apply it to a large-scale nuclear attack. He states his conclusions in the following passage:

> ...the current strategy of NATO has veered realistically towards a "counter-force' attack directed against the enemy's nuclear striking power, missile stores, launching sites, etc. A massive attack on an area in which these are located could well be justified by the principle of double effect, even with heavy incidental loss of innocent lives.
>
> It is impossible to be as precise about the degree of incidental havoc of other kinds, including, in particular, contamination of the atmosphere with radio-active elements liable to cause sickness and death in the explosion area and evil genetic effects elsewhere, which would be such as to render the use, or further use, of nuclear weapons morally illicit. Widespread devastation and atmospheric contamination could result from the use of nuclear weapons , even if they were used exclusively on legitimate military objectives. In that case, their use could not be justified by the principle of double effect unless the good to be preserved by such a form of self-defence were great enough to outweigh the incidental and, we presume, unwanted evil side-effects. One cannot demonstrate a priori that it could never do so. It is admittedly difficult to imagine any temporal good sufficient to do so, but the spiritual good of preserving the world from atheistic domination is great enough to compensate for many temporal evils that might be incidental to achieving it.[24]

---

[23] Ramsey, Just War, pp. 350, 355.

[24] McReavy, Peace, pp. 46-47.

This passage illustrates that the application of the principle of double effect defies precise analysis, particularly when the vast and hypothetic case of nuclear war is discussed. My discussion below of the just war criterion of proportionality will further illustrate some of the issues which also apply to proportionality within the principle of double effect.

We have noted two arguments counterforce advocates use to refute nuclear pacifism while upholding the principle of discrimination: there may be circumstances in which nuclear weapons can be used with little or no harm to noncombatants and even large-scale collateral damage may be justified by the principle of double effect. A third argument completes the logical progression: occasional war crimes do not invalidate an otherwise just war. L.L. McReavy states that: "It is true that, even in a just war, no immoral means may be used, but it does not necessarily follow that a just war in which immoral means are sometimes employed ceases itself to be justified."[25] He notes that the indiscriminate bombing of enemy cities by the Allies was a crime but did not remove all "title to fight the aggressor." Therefore he refutes Watkins' conclusion:

> Even granting, therefore, that nuclear weapons are likely to be used immorally in a future war (though they could be used morally), one cannot automatically conclude that 'it is under any circumstances utterly immoral to participate in any way in the preparation, still less in the employment of such weapons or in any war which employs them'.[26]

---

[25]L.L. McReavy, "The Debate on the Morality of Future War," Clergy Review, VL (1960), 83.

[26]Ibid. Reference is to Watkin, "Unjustifiable War," p. 62.

In response to such an argument Walter Stein admits that perhaps the "abuses" of World War II did not invalidate the war, though this is uncertain because the massacre of obliteration bombing became war policy. However, when it comes to the nuclear stockpile, with its "overkill" capacity, "abuse is its only conceivable _raison d'être_."[27]

---

[27]Stein, _Peace on Earth_, p. 27.

The Criterion of Proportionality

Besides discrimination, the second key just war criterion used by nuclear pacifists is that of proportionality. In the just war tradition the term may be used to require that punishment be proportionate to guilt or that the value of a given military action be proportionate to the damage it does. I will be using the word in its most general sense, however: the good achieved by a war must outweigh the evil consequences produced by fighting it. Already in 1933 Fr. Ryan, quoting Pope Pius XI, concluded that "modern war, a means so 'monstrously murderous and almost certainly suicidal,' is not to be justified by any known and proportionate just cause."[28] With the advent of the nuclear era the case was made all that much stronger. Walter Stein is typical of nuclear pacifists in stating that nuclear warfare "could hardly achieve a just balance of consequences" for its evils "...might extend to the entire destruction of civilization, grave and permanent harm to future generations, and, potentially, even the total extermination of our species..."[29] E.I. Watkin states that:

---

[28] Ryan, "Modern War," p. 82.

[29] Stein, NWCC, p. 29. Stein says that such consequences could never be considered "unintended effects" justified by the principle of double effect. Donald Bloesch states that a nuclear war "would mean the certain end of civilization as we know it." A fairly large remnant would probably survive, but only "in the midst of misery and anarchy": "The age following an atomic war would be another dark age; it would be marked by a reversion to the law of the jungle." Bloesch, "The Christian," pp. 322-323.

> No cause however just, however important the
> issue, however great the value to be achieved
> by victory, can justify such diabolism, or
> should we rather call it criminal lunacy. No
> end however excellent can justify means so
> flagrantly immoral.[30]

In reaching these conclusions nuclear pacifists judge or assume that
it is unlikely that nuclear war could be kept limited. First, they simply
believe the government threats of "massive retaliation" and expect that
nuclear war will assume that shape.[31] Secondly, as I will show in Chapter
4, they believe that our announced reliance on a deterrent policy of
mutual assured destruction erodes the possibility of restraint in a
situation of actual war. Thirdly, they state that there may be loss of
command and control in a nuclear war.[32]

While other nuclear pacifists judge that nuclear war would
(probably) be disproportionate, Francis Winters, S.J., also states that
the very fact of the unpredictability of nuclear war renders it incapable
of moral justification:

> Literally no one knows what a nuclear war would
> be like....The unknowability of the potential
> damage precludes any effort to ask one of the
> essential moral questions about a prospective
> war: What is the proportion between loss and

----

[30]Watkin, "Unjustifiable War," p. 52.

[31]Stein, NWCC, pp. 34-35.

[32]Francis Winters cites a United States Arms Control and Disarmament
Agency report that electronic control may be disrupted in nuclear war.
Francis Winters, "The Nuclear Arms Race: Machine vs. Man," Ethics and
Nuclear Strategy?, ed. Harold Ford and Francis Winters (Maryknoll, New
York, 1977), p. 145. Hereafter cited as Ford and Winters, ENS?.

> gain to be expected from the hostilities?
> If the losses are unpredictable, no calcu-
> lation of their proportionality to political
> gains is feasible; hence, policy planners and
> political leaders are unable to certify the
> preponderance of gain over loss.[33]

Thus according to Winters one cannot even begin to apply the principle

of proportionality to nuclear war, but other nuclear pacifists judge that

in its probable shape nuclear war is so disproportionate that it is

irrational: it can serve no useful purpose because it destroys what it

seeks to save. Thus nuclear war fails to meet another of the just war

criteria: there must be reasonable hope of victory (winability), other-

wise the evil of war is simply added to the evil of injustice rather than

preventing the injustice. As Watkin says, "What hope of victory can there

be in a war which, even in the present development of nuclear weapons,

must prove the mutual suicide of both parties?"[34] In short, when it

comes to nuclear war, the immoral and the irrational merge and together

become demonic; thus in the previous quotation from Watkin, (n. 30) "dia-

bolism" and "criminal lunacy" are the two names for nuclear war.

The principle of proportionality states that in order for a war

to be just more good must be achieved (or evil avoided) than there is

evil done. Therefore to avoid a nuclear pacifist conclusion a writer

---

[33]Ford and Winters, ENS?, p. 146. At the same time, Winters goes on
to cite studies which show that even the predictable (as opposed, apparently, to the unpredictable) results of all-out nuclear war would include
over 200 million fatalities; the destruction of much of the earth's ozone
layer, with "truly apocalyptic consequences"; and the destruction of so
many non-renewable resources that our present industrial civilization
could not be rebuilt--all effects which in his judgment are beyond moral
justification (pp. 147-148).

[34]Watkin, "Unjustifiable War," p. 52.

may offer a different assessment of either side of the equation. Various means have been used to weight the side of the good to be achieved. Theodore Weber concedes that submission to communism would not be so bad as a major nuclear exchange, and that therefore the evil effects of nuclear war negate the finaltraditional just cause, the right of national self-defense against aggression. Rather than adopting nuclear pacifism, however, he simply raises the stakes: American nuclear deterrence (with its risk of nuclear war) can (only) be justified as a means of preserving the total international order. The nuclear powers have the "office" of preventing aggression, thereby preventing insecurity and nuclear prolif- eration among the non-nuclear powers.[35]

While Weber stresses political values, others emphasize the moral and spiritual values at stake in opposing the communist enemy. Paul Crane refutes two of the nuclear pacifists writing in Morals and Missiles, Christopher Hollis, who argues that self-defense means the defense of institutions, which would be destroyed in war, and E.I. Watkin. After noting that controlled nuclear war is possible, he says:

> But, secondly and most importantly, we must
> not confine ourselves to a material standard
> when weighing the damage brought by a just war
> against that which comes from permitted
> aggression. Moral and spiritual values must
> be thrown into the balance at this point. With
> respect to Mr. Hollis, defence in international
> affairs means a great deal more than "the
> defence of institutions." It must include the
> upholding of values. There are worse things
> than physical death and destruction, and
> slavery can be one of them. With respect to

---

[35]Weber, MWPP, pp. 14-15, 31-32.

> Mr. Watkin, I would suggest that the spiritual
> good represented by "freedom from the tyranny
> of the Communist state" is not too hardly won
> even at the cost of material death and destruc-
> tion in nuclear form. Indeed, the primacy of
> the spiritual can be such as to turn failure
> into success, defeat into victory. A nation is
> not necessarily wrong if it takes up arms to
> defend what is, on a materialist calculation,
> a hopeless cause; yet knowing that its heroic
> and devastating defeat will enshrine forever in
> a world that needs them values without which no
> people can really live.[36]

It appears that by such calculation hardly any kind of destruction could

outweigh the moral and spiritual values presumed involved in the East/

West struggle, and because of this the criterion of winability is deemed

irrelevant. The thought is repeated in more graphic form by Robert Paul

Mohan, S.S., when he discusses the "temptation to consider capitulation

with an attempt at consequent conversion as preferable to extinction at

the hands of the Soviets." While he recognizes that the democracy-com-

munism conflict is not simply a struggle of God and anti-God, Mohan

concludes: "But as one who considers capitulation to communism equivalent

to extinction, I would prefer smashed buildings and smashed skulls as

preferable to a Soviet world without God and freedom."[37] Crane and

perhaps also Mohan at least expect the world to go on if the United States

is destroyed. Nuclear pacifists, as we have noted, are not so sure that

---

[36]Crane, "Catholic," p. 27. Cf. also McReavy, Peace, pp. 46-47,
n. 24 above.

[37]Robert Paul Mohan, "Thermonuclear War and the Christian," Christian
Ethics and Nuclear Warfare, ed. Ulrich Allers and William O'Brien
(Washington, D.C., 1961), p. 76.

that would be the case.

There are other critics of nuclear pacifism who rather than tipping the scales in favor of the good to be achieved or evil avoided by nuclear war adopt the other approach of claiming that effects of such a war need not be as bad as nuclear pacifists claim. Ernest Lefever criticizes some who "tend to expect the worst in the event of hostilities" and "tend to exaggerate that worst." He notes that:

> According to the best projections available the maximum possible loss of life from a general nuclear war involving the full present capacities of the Soviet Union and the United States would be about twenty percent of the earth's population. The number killed might well be considerably less. There would be practically no casualties of any kind south of the equator.[38]

At the same time Lefever argues that "Such a war is probably the least likely contingency, but it seems to be the only contingency that the neo-pacifists talk about. It is possible, perhaps probable, that World War III will be less destructive than World War II, or even than World War I."[39]

It is striking, however, that most counterforce moralists express little hope that nuclear war can be kept limited. In responding to Lefever Paul Ramsey remarks that, "Those who say it may not be possible

---

[38]Ernest Lefever, "Facts, Calculation and Political Ethics," The Moral Dilemma of Nuclear Weapons (New York, 1961), p. 41. Hereafter cited as Lefever, "Calculation." John C. Bennett challenges his conclusions, though not his method, in "Ethics and 'Calculation'," The Moral Dilemma of Nuclear Weapons, pp. 44-46.

[39]Lefever, "Calculation," p. 42.

for us to limit warfare are <u>almost</u> certainly correct."[40] Similarly,

L.L. McReavy states that a controlled nuclear war is possible; "Such,

however, is human folly, that a war begun in restraint is very likely to

end in uncontrolled and therefore immoral violence, even on the part of

the just defender."[41] For counterforce theorists then, who are writing

in a time when, except for the interlude of McNamara's 1962 initiative,

the central policy is that of mutual assured destruction, the ethical

problem of nuclear war is how to <u>create</u> the possibility of limited war.

This is best stated by John Courtney Murray, S.J.:

> First, there are those who say that the limitation
> of nuclear war, or any war, is today impossible,
> for a variety of reasons--technical, political, etc.
> In the face of this position, the traditional doc-
> trine simply asserts again, 'The problem today is
> limited war.' But notice that the assertion is on
> a higher plane than that of sheer fact. It is a
> moral proposition, or better, a moral imperative.
> In other words, since nuclear war may be a necessity,
> it must be made a possibility. Its possibility
> must be created.[42]

Counterforce moralists state three ways in which war may be kept

limited and thus (perhaps) proportionate. First, counterforce targeting

if observed would itself limit the destruction of nuclear war. Paul

---

[40]Paul Ramsey, "Right and Wrong Calculation," <u>The Moral Dilemma of
Nuclear Weapons</u> (New York, 1961), p. 53. Hereafter cited as Ramsey,
"Calculations."

[41]L.L. McReavy, "The Morality of Nuclear Warfare," <u>The Tablet</u>, CCXI
(1958), 294.

[42]Murray, <u>MMW</u>, p. 18.

Ramsey complains after Secretary McNamara's speech of June, 1962, that
public opinion has ignored the quantitative and qualitative differences
between killing 25,000,000 people in an all-out counterforce war and
killing 215,000,000 people in an all-out countercity war.[43] Secondly,
war must be limited to reasonable political objectives. It cannot be a
deadly contest of wills between commanders[44] nor the mentality of "better
dead than red" as represented above by Crane and Mohan. Thus it must be
specified in the nuclear age that the criterion of winability means "a
reasonable hope of reasonable victory, not of an irrational one."[45] This
leads directly to a third requirement: surrender is preferable to the
annihilation of ourselves and/or the enemy. As Ramsey puts it: "...
either side should be prepared to stop if it seems likely that war will
escalate into a purposeless use of violence."[46] To continue the war in
such a case would be, according to Murray, "worse than injustice; it
would be sheer folly."[47]

It is clear from this discussion that there is no one "scale" on
which to weigh the good and evil consequences of war, even if they could

-----

[43]Ramsey, Just War, p. 213. Cf. also Ramsey, "Calculation," p. 53.

[44]Ramsey, Just War, pp. 223-224.

[45]Ramsey, Just War, p. 357. Cf. also Murray, MMW, pp. 16-17.

[46]Ramsey, Just War, p. 357.

[47]Murray, MMW, p. 17.

be clearly predicted. Ramsey notes that politics and ethics are inexact
sciences and that proportionality especially is based on intuitive judgment.[48] Winters in discussing counterforce warfare notes that there is
no precise consensus on a morally acceptable level of collateral civilian
damage, but he offers the figure of the holocaust of the Jews, six million,
as surely unacceptable to most critics--and shows that a counterforce
attack on the U.S. would exceed that figure.[49] Nuclear pacifists and most
counterforce advocates agree that all-out nuclear war would be immoral.
One of their most basic disagreements is whether it is right to take that
risk for the sake of fighting and deterring nuclear war.

[48]Ramsey, Peace, Churches, Bomb, pp. 61-62. He complains that
despite this fact nuclear pacifists especially make absolute statements.

[49]Ford and Winters, ENS?, pp. 150-151.

Other Just War Criteria

While the heart of the nuclear pacifist position is the judgment
that modern war fails to meet the criteria of discrimination and proportionality (along with winability), modern-war pacifists occasionally reach
that conclusion on the basis of other criteria as well. John K. Ryan
argues in "Modern War and Basic Ethics" (pp. 52-53, 70-76, 103) that war
today cannot meet the criteria of just cause and right intention as set
down in the Roman Catholic scholastic tradition. His discussion of just
cause may be summarized by these points: (1) Modern war is essentially
offensive or aggressive in character, because its decisive weapons are
made for attack rather than defense (73). (2) Subjective certainty of
just cause is required to justify offensive war (72). (3) Due to the
complexity of modern nations (71) and the vastness (71) and aggressive
character (73-74) of modern war, it can hardly be determined which side
is acting in unjust aggression and which side in just self-defense.
(4) Thus we cannot be certain that our side is just in any modern war
(74). (5) Therefore no modern war can be determined to be just according
to the demands of natural law (76).

Ryan bases his argument largely on the experience of World War I,
for years of discussion have produced no consensus on who was to blame
for it (71-72). He goes on to claim that today there can be no genuinely
right intention, for this depends partially on the sure knowledge that
one's cause is just (103).

Fr. Ryan also argues in an interesting way that modern war violates
the criterion of last resort (pp. 59-69, 104). In the scholastic theory,

peace was the normal condition of society and war was an abnormal and infrequent measure. Modern war, however, requires:

> ...universal conscription, the diversion of much, or even most, of the national income to the purposes of past, present and future wars, the dedication of science and invention, of education and even religion to the cause of the nation's military interests. In brief, the modern concept and fact of the nation in arms necessarily involve the organization of all the nation's resources in men and material as a permanent and effective machine for waging war. (pp. 60-61)

War is thus seen as inevitable and preparation for it is permanent. According to Ryan, the abnormal has become the normal and there is no true peace: "It is evident that as a continuing and universal process modern war has lost its claim to justification as a last resort." (p. 69)[50]

Besides the criteria discussed by Ryan, the traditional just war theory also required the observance of what may be called a "due form" of communication with the enemy during the initation and continuation of hostilities. Helmut Gollwitzer observes that this is threatened by the aims and weapons of modern war:

> ...the modern theory of the just war recognized the enemy's right to live, and to exist as a sovereign state. The rules of warfare and the weapons used were in accordance with this theory; so were the hostilities which were always preceded by warnings, by a solemn declaration of war, and in which battles alternated with periods of respite so that diplomacy was never completely paralyzed and there was always opportunity, for contacts,

---

[50] It is not hard to imagine what Ryan would think of the great powers today! Michael Novak entitled a recent article on the East/West conflict, "We Are Already at War" (Notre Dame Magazine, May, 1980, pp. 14-16).

> negotiations, and for the official inter-
> vention of neutrals.
>   The new weapons, on the other hand, have
> only one purpose: to take the enemy by sur-
> prise and annihilate him.[51]

Gollwitzer points out by this contrast that the observance of due form in

the conduct of hostilities was not simply a procedural matter but involved

an attitude of respect for the rights of the enemy. That respect is threat-

ened not only by the destructive power of nuclear weapons but by the speed

and range of their delivery vehicles.[52]

Since most nuclear pacifists do not adopt the specific arguments

raised by Ryan and Gollwitzer, the points they raise have sparked little

controversy. Most nuclear pacifists assume that just cause for war may

still be determined. Paul Ramsey does de-emphasize just cause because it

is difficult for most people to ascertain, but rather than question the

validity of war like Ryan does he simply takes right conduct in war to be

the essence of the just war tradition.[53] Other nuclear pacifists do

---

[51]Helmut Gollwitzer, "Christian Commitment," Therefore Choose Life
(London, 1961), p. 37.

[52]Richard Thaxton notes that today missiles from Soviet submarines
can hit targets in the U.S. in as few as three minutes from first
detection, fostering a U.S. "launch-on warning" mentality. Richard
Thaxton, "Nuclear War by Computer Chip: How America Almost 'Launched
on Warning'," The Risk of the Cross (New York, 1981), p. 66. Joseph
McKenna, S.J., discusses the compressed warning time in case of attack
as a problem for the requirements that an injury be real and thus known
for certain and that war be a last resort. He concludes that these
criteria would allow a counterattack in the case of a full-scale nuclear
attack. Joseph McKenna, "Ethics and War: A Catholic View," American
Political Science Review, LIV (1960), 647-658.

[53]E.g. Ramsey, WCC, pp. 32-33.

discuss the militarization of society, as I will show in Chapter 4, but they do not relate it to the criterion of last resort as does Ryan. Most just war theorists are little concerned about questions of due form in relation to nuclear war, though as I noted above Murray and Ramsey do at least assume that there will be opportunity for surrender in a nuclear war. On the other hand just war moralists are very concerned with right intention, but in connection with the principle of noncombatant immunity, rather than as a separate criterion concerning the aims and attitudes of war. In fact, in the main stream of the debate the question of intention arises not only in discussing war but in discussing deterrence, which is supposed to prevent war. It is to the whole issue of nuclear deterrence that we turn in the next chapter.

Chapter III

THE MORALITY OF NUCLEAR DETERRENCE

The Issue of Nuclear Deterrence

In Chapter II I presented some of the arguments about whether it
could be moral to use nuclear weapons to fight in a projected war. However, that issue can never be wholly separated from the question of
whether it is moral to use nuclear weapons to deter an enemy from engaging
in or escalating armed conflict. In some ways the issue of deterrence is
the more pressing one because unlike nuclear war the deterrence system
based on nuclear weapons is a present, ongoing reality involving not only
the nuclear powers but many of their allies as well.

Just what the relationship is between the two uses of nuclear weapons
is itself a matter of dispute. In this chapter I will describe the debate
between nuclear pacifism and two contending views of deterrence, the
counterforce theory and the bluff position. Since in the deterrence
debate nuclear pacifism begins with a negation of other views, in this
chapter I will give to the two opposing views the role of protagonist.

Those who hold the bluff position regard deterrence as a whole
different order of action from any war-fighting policy, and thus governed
by a different intention and norm. Nuclear pacifists and (at least
initially) counterforce theorists agree in opposition to this that there
is a unity between the intention to wage nuclear war and the intention to
threaten an enemy with it, though of course they differ radically on how
to evaluate that intention. Nuclear pacifists claim that since it would

be immoral to wage nuclear war, it is immoral to threaten it; counterforce advocates say that a nuclear war which may be fought may also be threatened --I will call this "counterforce deterrence." Counterforce theorists face a difficulty however. They refuse to condemn all nuclear war because some nuclear war could be moral; but deterrence policy is a present fact and therefore open to concrete evaluation. Since countercity retaliation has never been publicly repudiated as at least a part of official Western deterrence policy, even when counterforce targeting has been emphasized, it would seem that the current deterrence policy is immoral. L. L. McReavy does refer in passing to NATO's "policy of deterring aggression by threat of massive nuclear retaliation against enemy cities" as an "immoral threat",[1] but he and other counterforce advocates are reluctant to condemn the existing deterrent altogether. Therefore they employ various arguments, some of which bring them to or beyond the verge of abandoning a "pure" counterforce deterrence position in favor of allowing an element of "bluff" in deterrence. No one illustrates the tendency better than Paul Ramsey.

Since he has discussed issues of deterrence much more fully than other counterforce moralists, and since it is important to see the connections in his arguments, I will use Ramsey as the sole proponent of counterforce deterrence.

----

[1] L. L. McReavy, "The Debate on the Morality of Future War," Clergy Review, VL (1960), 87. Hereafter cited as McReavy, "Debate."

Paul Ramsey on Counterforce Deterrence

In 1961 Ramsey first dealt at length with the issue of deterrence in
his book, War and the Christian Conscience: How Shall Modern War Be Conducted Justly? (Durham, N.C., 1961). He revised some of his views in
the pamphlet The Limits of Nuclear War (New York, 1963). The symposium
Peace, the Churches and the Bomb (New York, 1965) contained three rounds
of discussion: several authors commented on Schema XIII of the Second
Vatican Council; Ramsey offered "More Unsolicited Advice to Vatican
Council II"; Theodore Weber, Walter Stein, Justus George Lawler and William
O'Brien responded to Ramsey. Never one to leave the scene of an argument,
Ramsey responded in the booklet Again, The Justice of Deterrence (New
York, 1965) which was included along with a number of Ramsey's other
articles on deterrence in The Just War: Force and Political Responsibility
(New York, 1968). The main lines of Ramsey's thought, as well as some of
the objections of his critics, may be brought out by discussing in turn
the four types of deterring effects which he distinguishes: damage to
military forces, collateral civilian damage, the uncertainty that weapons
will not be used against civilians, and the "bluff." Following Walter
Stein,[2] I will call these types A, B, C, and D respectively.

The theme of War and the Christian Conscience in regard to deterrence
is that the only moral and effective deterrent is a counterforce deterrent.
A country's deter-the-war policy must be based on its fight-the-war policy,
otherwise the enemy will (rightly) judge it in-credible that the threat
will be carried out. The only fight-the-war policy that is moral and

---

[2]Stein, Peace, Churches, Bomb, p. 79.

politically purposive is a counterforce policy. Ramsey tends to think
that there is no need for nuclear weapons as large as those used on Hiroshima and Nagasaki (p. 292), and doubts that there is _any_ just use for
megaton weapons (pp. 167, 292, 320). No moralist alone can determine
counterforce targeting needs, but at least the larger megaton weapons and
nearly all of our stockpile of smaller megaton weapons should be disman-
tled, unilaterally if need be (pp. 299-301). In the meantime, it should
be announced by the government that any war would be fought only by
counterforce measures: "Not to announce would be deceit; and worse, for
it is surely immoral even to leave standing an assumption that one may
use immoral means." (p. 165)

In this view then the ability and intention to destroy an enemy's
military forces in the event of war, if necessary with nuclear weapons,
is sufficient to deter war in the first place. Subsequently Ramsey
expanded his analysis in two directions. First he noted that deterrence
operated not only prior to war to prevent it, but also within war to keep
it from going to higher levels of violence. Secondly, and more importantly
for our purposes here, Ramsey identified three other types of deterrent
effect of nuclear weapons. Beyond the threat of the destruction of
military forces themselves, the next level of deterrence (type B) depends
upon the "collateral civilian damage" which would attend counterforce
nuclear actions:

> The collateral civilian damage that would
> result from counterforces warfare in its maximum
> form may itself be quite sufficient to deter either
> side from going so high and to preserve the rules
> and tacit agreements limiting conflict in a nuclear
> age. In that case, deterrence during the war and
> collateral civilian damage are both "indirect
> effects" of a plan and action of war which would

> be licit or permitted by the traditional rules
> of civilized conduct in war....Collateral
> civilian damage is certainly an unavoidable
> indirect effect and, in the technical sense,
> an "unintended" result of something a nation
> may and should make itself conditionally
> willing and ready to do. The deterrent effect,
> of which we are now speaking, is then, as it
> were, an indirect effect of the foreseeable
> indirect effects of legitimate military con-
> duct.[3]

In _Peace, the Churches and the Bomb_ Walter Stein criticizes this
statement as "a radical abuse of double-effect categories" (p. 80), for
double effect deals with "<u>radically unwanted</u>" effects which are not a
means to an end: "The decisive flaw in Ramsey's position is the dependence
of his supposed 'collateral deterrence' upon effects essential to the purpose of nuclear strategy, directly indispensable, radically wanted--and
yet to be sanctioned as '<u>side-effects</u>.'" "No wonder," says Stein, that
is the last sentence quoted above, "Ramsey's language shows signs of
stumbling" (p. 81).

Dr. Ramsey answers Stein in _Again, the Justice of Deterrence,_[4] for
"a great deal depends upon the outcome of this debate, no matter how many
don't care." (p. 315) He admits that his language was misleading; the
deterrent effect is a <u>direct</u> effect of the <u>indirect</u> and unavoidable
collateral civilian damage which would result from a counterforce nuclear
war. The deterrent effect may and should be wanted, while the death of
noncombatants on which it rests is radically unwanted. However, Ramsey
does not say that whether the death of civilians is a wanted means to an
end and thus a violation of the principle of double effect, as Stein claims,

---

[3] Ramsey, _Just War_, p. 252.

[4] New York, 1965. Pages cited from Ramsey, _Just War_, pp. 314-366. The
following paragraph summarizes Ramsey's argument in _Just War_, pp. 315-328.

is merely a matter of subjective desire. The objective criterion is that no further civilian harm may be planned for the sake of deterrence than would be necessary to actually fight a just counterforce war. Otherwise the principle of double effect would be violated and one would have a murderous intention (p. 318). But, according to Ramsey, if there is no extension of the target, it is perfectly legitimate to use anticipated collateral damage in a scheme of mutual deterrence (p. 325).

The third type of deterrence (type C) which Ramsey discusses results from the uncertainty inherent in any possession of nuclear weapons: "No matter how often we declare, and quite sincerely declare, that our targets are an enemy's forces, he can never be quite _certain_ that in the fury or in the fog of war his cities may not be destroyed."[5] The point is that "in a nuclear age all war raises a risk of general war by an apparent _possibility_ of a _politically_ _irreversible_ _trend_. War creates this risk which we share with the Russians."[6] The ineradicability of this type of deterrence

> ...is so certainly the case that the problem
> of how to deter an enemy from striking our
> cities ought not for one moment to impede
> the shift to a counter-forces policy and to
> the actual intentions to use nuclear weapons
> only against forces. We should declare again
> and again, and give evidence by what we do,
> that our targets are his forces rather than
> his cities.[7]

---

[5] Ramsey, _Just War_, p. 253. Cf. also Ramsey, _Peace, Churches, Bomb_, p. 52.

[6] Ramsey, _Just War_, p. 254.

[7] _Ibid._, p. 253.

Ramsey does not here specify what is the "evidence" of an actual counterforce policy, but in Peace, the Churches and the Bomb (p. 53) he "almost" agrees with Justus George Lawler that deterrence based on the ambiguity of weapons could be licit "only if the number of weapons in a nation's arsenal were sufficient to destroy nothing but an enemy's military strength."[8] Ramsey agrees if this is considered a judgment of proportionality within the limits of noncombatant immunity (as opposed, apparently, to an absolute noncombatant immunity) and if "Lawler does not mean to deny that a political-military leader has to make a prudent calculation within an ample margin of error or failure".[9] However, Ramsey seems to flatly contradict this limitation on nuclear stockpiles when he goes on to discuss the fourth kind of deterrence which is based on the bluff (see below).[10]

Walter Stein makes two criticisms of Ramsey's type C deterrence. The most important is that it is wrong even to risk general war:

> For, quite apart from 'intention,' it is
> immoral to make oneself responsible for
> actions and circumstances that could (one
> knows) uncontrollably lead to reciprocal
> genocide; and it is immoral to participate
> in preliminary activities (those of the peace-
> time deterrence set-up) that could, uncon-
> trollably, release the uncontrollable spiral
> of--'illimitable'--'limited war.'[11]

[8]Lawler, Peace, Churches, Bomb, p. 34.

[9]Ramsey, Peace, Churches, Bomb, p. 53.

[10]Lawler notes this "reversal of position" and "contradiction" in Peace, Churches, Bomb, p. 90. Ramsey does not directly address the charge in Again, the Justice of Deterrence.

[11]Stein, Peace, Churches, Bomb, p. 83, author's italics.

Secondly, just as in type B deterrence, "the menace to populations is essential, indispensable, morally wanted for the purposes of our strategy," though in this case it is only a "threat by default" since we risk what we cannot control.[12]

In his rebuttal[13] Ramsey does not again address the question of what is "wanted", but he does make clear that this type of deterrence remains even though the government has removed as much risk from it as possible (p. 331). In assessing risk, Ramsey adopts a principle used by United States courts in free-speech cases that the gravity of an evil must be discounted by its improbability (pp. 331-332). He notes that he was discussing only an "apparent possibility" of a "politically irreversible trend" that would escalate a limited war to general war--" a far cry from an actually irreversible trend..." (p. 332). And while he does not deny that the evil of general war would be very grave, Ramsey believes that "peace, justice, and security" depend upon deterrence (p. 332). I would briefly paraphrase Ramsey this way: the great evil of all-out (countervalue) nuclear war may be risked for the great goods achieved by deterrence as long as the risk is not too high and steps are taken to reduce the risk. While type C deterrence is at issue here, this argument might apply to all types of nuclear deterrence, and Ramsey himself applies it to the bluff (p. 332).

---

[12]Ibid.
[13]Ramsey, _Just War_, pp. 328-333.

The Nuclear Bluff as a Deterrent

The second and third types of deterrent effects discussed above
represent a new emphasis for Paul Ramsey but not a departure from his
position in War and the Christian Conscience. The case is different in
regard to the fourth type, however. In WCC Ramsey stressed that it would
be ineffective not to base deterrence on a counterforce policy and immoral
not to declare that we would only fight counterforce warfare (see above).
Later, however, he questioned both ideas when he allowed that it might be
legitimate to bluff, that is, to threaten what it would be immoral to
actually do.[14]   In The Limits of Nuclear War he states: "If [deterrence
types B and C] do not seem to the military analyst sufficiently persuasive,
or able to be made so, then an apparent resolution to wage war irrationally
or at least an ambiguity about our intentions may have to be our expressed
policy."[15] Just as the two main criteria by which nuclear weapons policy
is challenged are those of discrimination and proportionality, so Ramsey
offers "the deterrence of bluff or ambiguity"[16] (type D) as a way to avoid
objections on both counts. He discusses each type of bluff independently
without much effort to relate them. The first type of bluff is a deterrence
policy which threatens civilian populations in apparent violation of the
principle of noncombatant immunity.

Dr. Ramsey admits[17] that a policy of bluff or ambiguity would be a
form of deception, but it would not be a lie, since it is doubtful that

---

[14]Ramsey, Just War, pp. 254-258, 333-336, 358-366; Ramsey, Peace,
Churches, Bomb, pp. 50-52, 55-58. Ramsey acknowledges his change of mind
in Peace, Churches, Bomb, p. 44, note 3; Just War, pp. viii-ix.

[15]Ramsey, Just War, p. 254, author's italics. Ramsey himself renders no
judgment on whether such a policy is necessary.

[16]Ramsey, Just War, p. 334.

[17]This paragraph is based on Ramsey, "The Limits of Nuclear War," in
Just War, pp. 255-257.

the enemy is "owed" information about our true intentions, particularly if telling the truth would result in war (p. 256). Even if such intent to deceive were wrong, it would not be nearly as bad as the conditional intent to do murder which would be involved in an actual intention to strike cities (p. 257). On balance, according to Ramsey, such a policy is both "morally 'do-able'" and politically and militarily feasible (p. 257). However, he remains uncomfortable enough with such a policy that if at all possible the other two types of deterrence (B and C) should be made to work so that this type is unnecessary (pp. 256-257). In fact, by 1972 Ramsey says briefly of deterrence from a "bluffing" possession of nuclear weapons: "I now think that an input of deliberate ambiguity about the counter-people use of nuclear weapons is not possible unless it is (immorally) meant and not a very good idea in the first place."[18] Thus, just as in his earlier two stages of thought (War and the Christian Conscience and Peace, Churches, Bomb (Just War), Ramsey believes that the moral and strategic requirements of nuclear deterrence coincide.

Ramsey's main concern above was to show that the explicit or ambiguous threat of willingness to attack cities need not involve a murderous intention, which would render such form of deterrence presently and inherently immoral. But it is also possible to threaten counterforce action so vast that, while observing the principle of discrimination, it would violate the principle of proportionality. In fact, Ramsey agrees with William O'Brien that in "modern deterrence" "disproportionate (in terms of traditional military utility) threats are seemingly the indis-

---

[18]See Paul Ramsey, "The MAD Nuclear Policy," Worldview, XV (1972), 18.

pensable means of avoiding general war".[19]   Therefore as noted above
Ramsey seems to abandon his agreement with Lawler, that a government may
possess only those nuclear weapons with legitimate counterforce uses, when
he allows a disproportionate bluff.

Dr. Ramsey admits that if the threat of military action that would be
disproportionate if it were carried out involved the actual conditional
intention to carry it out, the present intention (and thus modern
deterrence) would be immoral (p. 56). However, the "deterrent intention
terminates rather in the prevention of the grave evil of general war and
in the enforcement of limits upon any actual outbreak of hostilities (pp.
56-57). To use my terms, the deterrent threat is a political act and the
good and evils to be weighed are of the political realm; thus the threat
is separated from the thing threatened, which is a military act with its
own good and evil consequences. Each of these two realms has its own
scale of proportionality and that is why "A threat of something disproportionate [in the military realm] is not necessarily a disproportionate
threat [in the political realm]." (p. 55) Because war is so evil, threats
to prevent its initiation or escalation "may justifiably go quite high"
(p. 56). There is, however, one type of deterrence policy which would be
inherently disproportionate: any "rationality of irrationality" policies
in which escalating nuclear response is placed beyond human control.[20]

---

[19]William V. O'Brien, "After Nineteen Years, Let Us Begin," _Peace,
Churches, Bomb_, p. 30. Quoted in Ramsey, _Peace, Churches, Bomb_, p. 55.
The page references in the next paragraph are to Ramsey, _Peace, Churches,
Bomb_, pp. 55-59.

[20]Ramsey has in mind some sort of "Doomsday Machine" which would
automatically strike Soviet targets in the event of an attack in the
United States. Cf. Ramsey, _WCC_, pp. 260-268 and _Just War_, pp. 174-176.

(pp. 58-59) It is not clear from his brief discussion, but apparently
Ramsey means that such an action would be disproportionate for two reasons:
1) It would replace the "bluff" with an actual (conditioned) intention
(at the point of setting up the system) to do disproportionate harm; and
2) the "dehumanization of politics" would be such a great evil that no
objectives, including any amount of peace, could justify it (p. 59).

The most basic objection which nuclear pacifists make to the argument
from bluff especially in its countervalue form is that they simply do not
believe that the Western (particularly here the British and American)
governments are, in fact, bluffing. Stein begins his article, "Would You
Press the Button?,"[21] with a question which British Air Commodore Magill
was asked at the British Official Secrets Trial of 1962: "Would you press
the button you know is going to annihilate millions of people?" The
answer of Air Commodore Magill was "If the circumstances demanded it, I
would." (p. 20) Stein refuses to believe that the Air Commodore was
lying under oath (p. 22), and he sees this response as no surprise, for
"everybody knows that the backbone of nuclear strategy remains the threatened incineration of enemy cities" (20). He then marshalls five other
quotations to that effect from British and American military and political
leaders, including President Eisenhower and Secretary McNamara (p. 21).
In response Paul Ramsey makes a brief attempt to mitigate the countervalue
force of three of the statements, but the real point is that "one has
still to ask whether the intent need be real behind the words for there
to be more than enough deterrence" (p. 45). That question is to be set-

---

[21]
Stein, Peace, Churches, Bomb, pp. 20-25. Page references in this
paragraph will be to Peace, Churches, Bomb.

tled apart from what Eisenhower or McNamara themselves meant (p. 45).
Ramsey then goes on, as we have seen, to try to show that deterrent effects
of types B, C, and D may provide an effective nuclear deterrent without
any reliance on the actual intention to commit genocide or disproportionate
evil. It seems then that according to Ramsey intentionality is to be
judged by the objective needs of deterrence rather than by the subjective
intention of actual leaders.

Nuclear pacifists do not rest their case only on belief in the truth-
fulness of military and political leaders, however: they too have a view
on the objective needs of deterrence. They believe that in order to
effectively deter an enemy, nuclear threats must be actually intended by
at least some members of society. Thus a threat to attack an enemy's
cities must be either immoral or ineffective, and since they assume that
the government would not want an ineffective deterrent, it must be immoral.
Stein argues in this way: Even if an American President or British Prime
Minister secretly resolved never to carry out retaliation against cities,
this could not be communicated to military personnel handling the weapons
without the enemy finding out (p. 22).[22] Even if this could be done,

> ...by what national whispering campaign or
> telepathic proclamation, flawlessly shielded
> from the enemy, might the underlying innocence
> of the deterrence policy be conveyed to the
> rest of us--all of us, in whose name it is
> being carried out? Ultimately, in this matter
> of genocidal commitments, L'état c'est nous.
> It is possible for a Deterrence State to be

---

[22] Page references in this paragraph will be to Peace, Churches, Bomb.

> divided against itself; it is impossible that
> it should be secretly united in self-contra-
> diction. (p. 23)

By bringing at least some of its citizens to concur in an apparently

murderous policy, "such a government would be guilty of scandal, in the

strict theological sense--of authoritatively leading its own subjects into

a gravely sinful intentional consent." (p. 80)

In "Again, the Justice of Deterrence" Ramsey recognizes the force

of the questions raised by Stein:

> At this point, I would gladly complete the
> shift from minus-city-hostage-but-plus-deliberate
> ambiguity deterrence [type D] to collateral-
> deterrence-plus-inherent-uncertainty-only [types
> B and C], if I could forget the men in positions
> of political responsibility for all the order
> there is in the world and if I could reformulate
> the only question that is mine to answer: Have I,
> as a moralist, the right (if I could) to require
> this shift, this denial, of them? I have already
> said that the collateral damage and the irremovable
> uncertainties are a certainly moral deterrent,
> while the deterrence of which we are now speaking
> has only probably morality. The most basic reason
> for hesitatingly or subjectively reaching a
> conclusion justifying a deterrence based on studied
> ambiguity is that (as Lawler wrote) to be believable
> to an enemy this deterrent 'must also be believable
> to the ordinary citizen of the threatening nation'
> (p. 89).[23]

While Ramsey does not claim to entirely remove the objection of Stein and

Lawler to type D deterrence (p. 362), he protests that no more immoral

intention should be ascribed to citizens than necessary. In order for

---

[23]Ramsey, Just War, p. 362, author's italics. The quotation in the
last sentence is from Lawler, Peace, Churches, Bomb, p. 33 and repeated
on p. 89. Page references in the rest of the paragraph will be to Ramsey,
"Again, the Justice of Deterrence," in Just War.

this type of deterrence to be effective, the enemy need only believe that we _might_ be willing to destroy cities", not that we necessarily are willing (p. 362). This is all that citizens need believe too, and in fact government statements are ambiguous because along with making deterrent threats, leaders say that nuclear war would be "monumental foolishness". Thus a people is made as ambiguous as the government, not murderous (p. 363). Also, for a citizen to believe that the government might attack cities is not the same as to will that it do so, though he or she might have such a willingness and demand it of the government as well (p. 362). Until a citizen is required to support an actual genocidal intention by government leaders, he or she can say, "I will and intend not, it is true, what sometimes I hear you say, but that alone which should ever be willed by anyone or politically done in these matters." (p. 363) It seems then that according to Ramsey citizens can support an ambiguous _policy_ but actually _intend_ only to support counterforce actions.

In terms of disproportionate counterforce warfare, Ramsey seems to justify an explicit threat for the sake of deterrence. He does not attempt to delineate what might be allowed in terms of countervalue warfare: explicit threats (with or without other contradictory statements), implicit threats, failure to repudiate past threats, and so forth. A more recent advocate of the bluff position is Fr. J. Bryan Hehir.[24] He too does not specify what type of threat may be permitted. It does seem

---

[24]Hehir applies to his own view Ramsey's term "bluff" in Gessert and Hehir, _The New Nuclear Debate_, p. 92. I have not used his thought as a sample because he does not argue the case as fully as Ramsey. His major contributions (other than influencing American bishops!) are the idea that there is an institutional basis for the distinction between deterrence policy and strategic policy (_NND_, pp. 50-52) and the claim that the consequences of _changing_ from MAD to a counterforce deterrence policy must be weighed as well as the absolute merits of each policy (_NND_, pp. 67-68).

though that in recent years the American Catholic bishops have been coming to define a position based on the "possession" of nuclear weapons which rules out any explicit nuclear threat but stops short of nuclear pacifism.

The Position of the American Catholic Bishops

In their 1976 pastoral letter, "To Live in Christ Jesus," the United States Catholic Conference of Bishops made this brief but significant statement:

> With respect to nuclear weapons, at least those with massive destructive capability, the first imperative is to prevent their use. As possessors of a vast nuclear arsenal, we must also be aware that not only is it wrong to attack civilian populations but it is also wrong to threaten to attack them as part of a strategy of deterrence. We urge the continued development and implementation of policies which seek to bring these weapons more securely under control, progressively reduce their presence in the world, and ultimately remove them entirely.[25]

Any "bluff" based on explicit threats against civilians is here ruled out. As it stands the statement could support a counterforce position, but Cardinal John Krol in September, 1979, stated that "with few exceptions" the counterforce use of nuclear weapons "entail blast and radiation effects which are still morally unacceptable," and he went on to quote the Second Vatican Council's condemnation of indiscriminate destruction.[26]

With bluff and counterforces theories ruled out by the American bishops, it would seem that (strategic) nuclear pacifism, including unilateral (strategic) nuclear disarmament would be the only alternative. However, in his testimony before the Senate Foreign Relations Committee on behalf of the Second Strategic Arms Limitation Treaty (SALT II),

---

[25] United States Catholic Conference of Bishops, "The Pastoral Letter on Moral Values," Origins, VI (November 25, 1976), p. 368.
[26] Cardinal John Krol, "The Churches and Nuclear War," Origins, IX (September 27, 1979), p. 236.

Cardinal Krol quoted the 1976 statement and then interpreted it in a
way that stopped short of nuclear pacifism:

> The moral judgment of this statement is that
> not only the use of strategic nuclear weapons, but
> also the declared intent to use them involved in
> our deterrence policy is wrong. This explains the
> Catholic dissatisfaction with nuclear deterrence
> and the urgency of the Catholic demand that the
> nuclear arms race be reversed. It is of the utmost
> importance that negotiations proceed to meaningful
> and continuing reductions in nuclear stockpiles,
> and eventually, to the phasing out altogether of
> nuclear deterrence and the threat of mutual-assured
> destruction.
>   As long as there is hope of this occurring,
> Catholic moral teaching is willing, while negotiations
> proceed, to tolerate the possession of nuclear
> weapons for deterrence as the lesser of two evils.
> If that hope were to disappear, the moral attitude
> of the Catholic Church would almost certainly have
> to shift to one of uncompromising condemnation of
> both use and possession of such weapons.[27]

As stated by Cardinal Krol the American bishops are moving beyond the

distinction between the actual use and the threatened use of nuclear

weapons as posited by the bluff position to a distinction between the use

or threatened use on the one hand and the possession of nuclear weapons

on the other hand. One reason for this (temporary and provisional) tol-

erance of possession is so that the American nuclear arsenal may be used

to gain multilateral nuclear disarmament. If this were the only reason,

this might simply be a case of pragmatic nuclear pacifism. However,

possession is also tolerated because it provides present deterrence bene-

fits. On this count it seems that an implicit threat is allowed instead

---

[27] Cardinal John Krol, "SALT II: A Statement of Support," Origins,
IX (September 13, 1979), p. 197.

of an explicit threat, and the bishops have ruled out only one form of the bluff position.[28]

Since most of the nuclear pacifists in my sample wrote before the bishops made these statements, they give no specific comment on them.[29] However, they do react to more generalized statements of the bluff position which may approach the view of the bishops. For instance, an editorial in The Tablet of London states that "the purpose of nuclear weapons is to achieve disarmament, and in the meantime ensure that they will not be used."[30] Walter Stein counters that no ultimate purpose of the 30,000 megaton nuclear stockpile can justify its immoral intrinsic function, which is indiscriminate destruction.[31]

All of these issues of threat, intention, targeting, and so forth do not, of course, arise in a vacuum. Nuclear policy has extremely important consequences which are part of the ethical debate. It is to the debate about those consequences, particularly in the light of the East/West conflict, that we turn in the next chapter.

---

[28] Cardinal Krol asks whether explicit threats are really necessary to maintain an effective deterrent in "The Churches and Nuclear War," op. cit.

[29] An exception is Francis Winters, whom I will cite in Chapter IV.

[30] The Tablet, CCXVII, March 23, (1963), p. 302.

[31] Walter Stein, The Tablet, CCXVII (March 30, 1963), p. 348.

Chapter IV

CONSEQUENCES, COMMUNISM, AND ETHICAL REASONING

Policies and Consequences

Nuclear pacifists find the prospect of modern war so appalling that they urgently call upon the nations of the world to cooperate in finding ways to solve problems without a resort to arms. They see the need to establish peace and protect justice by means of international law and institutions which can enforce it. For example, A Christian Approach to Nuclear War succinctly affirms

> ...the need of surrender of some measure of
> sovereignty by modern nations and the estab-
> lishment of international law by consent
> backed by discriminate use of police force
> under the direction of the United Nations
> or some form of world government.[1]

Counterforce advocates do not generally disagree with the goal of establishing international law and world government, but they have much less hope that at least in the near future this can be sufficiently achieved to abrogate the right of nations to engage in just wars. For instance, in discussing recent papal documents, particularly Pacem in Terris, Paul Ramsey states that

---

[1] A Christian Approach to Nuclear War (New York, 1960), p. 5. Here-after cited as Christian Approach.

>...no amount or kind of <u>adumbration</u> of world
>public authorities that <u>should take</u> the place
>of the nation-state system can of itself with-
>draw the right of war. This can only be
>accomplished by an actual political reordering
>of the world, to which the papal teachings point,
>and can only <u>point</u>....the moral right to use
>force cannot go down faster than the public
>authority and enforcement of a world community
>is organized.[2]

What is most controversial about nuclear pacifism is that it does,
in fact, withdraw the right of (mass destruction) warfare in the present
even without a viable world government. The critics of nuclear pacifism
point out the disastrous consequences that they believe would follow from
unilateral disarmament. They say that hostile nations would have free
reign to exercise blackmail, military aggression, and tyranny. Among the
first to suffer would be small nations dependent upon Western military
power for their security. War, even nuclear war, would probably result.
Theodore Weber paints a bleak picture in speaking of:

>...the certainty that any attempt on the part
>of the United States to abdicate its position
>of power in the world (an unlikely occurrence
>in any case) would produce more serious inter-
>national tension and more likelihood of nuclear
>war than would the maintenance of its nuclear
>armaments in a state of wartime readiness. The
>fact which cannot be ignored is that United
>States military power is the most important
>stabilizing element in world politics. To be
>sure, that power sometimes is used arrogantly
>and foolishly, but it serves nevertheless to
>deter aggression and to relieve smaller and/or
>weaker states from the need to build up their
>own nuclear weapons systems. Any serious signs
>of intention to withdraw from that role would

---

[2]Ramsey, <u>Just War</u>, pp. 198-199. Author's italics.

place the Russians especially and also the
Chinese under enormous pressure and temptation
to improve their power positions even at the
risk of war, and it would set off a scramble
for nuclear weapons systems on the part of
states that could foresee the loss of their
protection. Before this could take place,
however, reactions within the United States
itself almost certainly would deliver the
military capacity of the country into the hands
of those persons most likely to make direct
and extensive uses of nuclear weapons. The
moral option of advocating unilateral disarmament on nuclear pacifist premises seems to be
discredited by the likelihood that it would
contribute to the evocation of precisely those
results which it intends to avoid.[3]

Weber's statement illustrates the fact that the debate about nuclear

weapons takes place on a stage set by the Cold War between East and West.

Others do not fear the specter of war as much as that of communist domina-

tion of the West. As I noted in the discussion of proportionality in

Chapter II, some writers go so far as to prefer destruction to communism--

"Better dead than red". Most counterforce advocates, however, take a less

extreme view of the communist threat. John Courtney Murray states that

just as the fact of the evil of modern war cannot be taken to its logical

conclusion of relative [i.e. nuclear] pacifism, neither can the fact that

communism poses a grave threat to the values of the West be taken to its

logical conclusion of "holy war".[4] Paul Ramsey too rejects both extreme

---

[3]Theodore Weber, Modern War and the Pursuit of Peace (New York, 1968),
p. 22. Hereafter cited as Weber, MWPP. James Dougherty in "The Christian
and Nuclear Pacifism," Catholic World, CXCVIII (1964), 345, also makes the
point that unilateral disarmament would lead to nuclear war. Hereafter
cited as Dougherty, "Nuclear Pacifism."

[4]John Courtney Murray, Morality and Modern War (New York, 1959), p.
5. Hereafter cited as Murray, MMW.

alternatives of "Better Dead or Better Red".[5] Most of the critics of
nuclear pacifism would agree with James Dougherty that Christians must
avoid believing either that the East is totally evil and the West is
totally good, or that the faults of the West are so great that both blocs
are equally evil. Instead, "we must hold to the belief that the political
and social values of the Western liberal civilization are superior to those
of the Communist system", and the difference is "vast" enough to justify
the risk of nuclear war.[6]

Nuclear pacifists are willing to argue the merits of various policies
in terms of their consequences. Their first point of course is that present
policies run a grave risk of nuclear war, and the consequences of nuclear
war would be more horrible than anything else that could be imagined.
However, they also respond directly to the concerns of their critics. Since
most of my sources predate the claims of Weber and Dougherty that unilateral nuclear disarmament would itself cause nuclear war, nuclear pacifists do not answer that specific charge. No doubt they assume that at
least any nuclear war would be less devastating than if the West retained
its nuclear weapons. Harold Fey is unflinchingly honest in this regard:
"Looking at the gloomy side, suppose our side scuttled or scattered its
nuclear weapons, and the communists attacked or destroyed us. The situation would still not be as bad as it would if we and the Russians were
to destroy each other."[7]

---

[5]Ramsey, Just War, p. 351. Ramsey in his work makes few explicit
references to communism.

[6]Dougherty, "Nuclear Pacifism," pp. 340-341.

[7]Harold Fey, "Fifteen Years in Hell is Enough," Christian Century,
LXXVII (1960), 892. That this editorial is written by Fey is affirmed by
the fact that it is reprinted under his name in God and the H-Bomb, ed.
Donald Keys (New York, 1961), pp. 64-67.

More positively, Fey states that "The removal of the threat from our side by unilateral nuclear disarmament would very likely result in the lessening of the threat from the communist side."[8] Most nuclear pacifists believe that a commitment to unilateral nuclear disarmament offers a better chance of both world peace and multilateral disarmament than does continued reliance on nuclear weapons. For instance, Norman Gottwald questions the "realism" of the "nuclear realism" which opposes "nuclear pacifism":

> Yet if realism means anything should it not
> take the measure of a myopic concern with arms
> that has crippled our will to search for
> alternative solutions and robbed our means
> to pay for them? Should not realism face the
> fact that the acceleration of weapons tech-
> nology and the spread of arms to other nations
> is not stabilizing the distribution of mili-
> tary power but staggering and scattering it
> erratically as we surge from one weapon system
> to another? The recent U-2 incident dramatically
> illustrates that the 'nuclear shield' is not a
> stabilizing factor in world affairs but tends
> rather to increase friction, stimulate chauvin-
> ism, and to multiply the chances of accidental
> disaster.[9]

By contrast, says Gottwald, "The nuclear pacifists believes that the renunication of unlimited force will allow--indeed virtually demand--a more accurate tracing of the roots of international chaos."[10] Also there might be great political import in a "unilateral renunciation of nuclear

---

[8] Ibid.

[9] Norman Gottwald, "Nuclear Realism or Nuclear Pacifism?," Christian Century, LXXVII (1960), 896-897. Hereafter cited as Gottwald, "NR or NP?".

[10] Ibid., p. 897.

weapons" by the United States: "could the Russians indefinitely resist

the attraction of favorable opinion by refusing to follow our lead?"[11]

Dr. Gottwald elsewhere suggests a "new defense policy" for the United

States which would include a series of unilateral "radical peace initatives"

such as a withdrawal of military bases from the borders of the Soviet

Union, the complete separation of conventional and nuclear weapons in the

armed forces, the establishment of a nuclear weapon-free zone in central

Europe, the transfer of part of the military budget to world development

projects, and the submission of international disputes to the World Court.

> The aims of such a program would be very tangible
> and unsentimental: (1) to seek to modify the
> extremely negative image of the U.S. in Russian
> eyes; (2) to grasp the political initiative so
> that hostile Russian political and military
> activity would be thrown off balance and ren-
> dered ineffectual; (3) to create the climate of
> relative trust in which bilateral agreements can
> be worked out.[12]

Walter Stein, too, sees no contradiction between unilateral and multi-

lateral action:

> Unilateralism as a commitment is, as we
> have repeatedly stressed, quite compatible
> with multilateral action...In the circumstances
> of our time even such exhilaratingly feasible
> programmes for multilateral progress as Arthur
> Waskow's will only be realised if at least some
> of the parties concerned commit themselves with
> an unconditional absoluteness to disarmament,

---

[11]Ibid., p. 898.

[12]Norman Gottwald, "Moral and Strategic Reflections on the Nuclear
Dilemma," Christianity and Crisis, XXI (1962), p. 241.

> including some form of last-resort--para-
> military or non-violent--defense. In such
> circumstances, protest and politics, prophecy
> and expediency, become imperatively inex-
> tricable.[13]

Despite such hopes for achieving peace and mutual disarmament, the question remains of what military posture of the West should assume if it had to dispose of its nuclear weapons unilaterally. Here nuclear pacifists are divided, at least in terms of emphasis. A few like Francis Winters believe that we need to find ways of defense and deterrence by conventional weapons, including such things as greatly built up NATO conventional forces.[14] By contrast, R. A. Markus assumes that without nuclear weapons "we could not, in the last resort, be militarily successful...". Therefore along with many other nuclear pacifists he urges Western governments to consider the methods of non-violent resistance[15] as developed by Gandhi and Martin Luther King, Jr.

---

[13] Walter Stein, Peace on Earth: The Way Ahead, ed. Walter Stein (London and Melbourne, 1966), p. 280. Hereafter cited as Stein, Peace on Earth. Waskow was one of the contributors to the volume.

[14] Francis Winters in Ethics and Nuclear Strategy?, ed. Harold Ford and Francis Winters (Maryknoll, N.Y., 1977), pp. 153-154. Hereafter cited as Ford and Winters, ENS?.

[15] R. A. Markus, "Conscience and Deterrence," in Nuclear Weapons and Christian Conscience, ed. Walter Stein (London, 1961), p. 86. Hereafter cited as Markus, "Conscience." Book hereafter cited as Stein, NWCC. It is not clear whether Norman Gottwald shifts his thinking or only his emphasis on this issue. In "NR or NP?' he speaks of nonviolent resistance but not conventional warfare (p. 898), while in "Moral and Strategic Reflections on the Nuclear Dilemma," Christianity and Crisis, XXI (1962), the reverse is true. In the latter it seems conventional forces will be maintained only during the period of the peace initiatives (p. 241), but it is not clear whether conventional forces would be maintained if the Soviet Union failed to respond to the initiatives (cf. p. 239).

The Conflict Between East and West

Those nuclear pacifists who do not hope that conventional military victory could be won seem to place the West in jeopardy of military domination vis-a-vis the Eastern bloc (apart from the question of the effectiveness of non-violent resistance). Therefore they offer further analysis of the nature of the struggle with communism. Some like Walter Stein de-absolutize the conflict by noting that the West is not very Christian[16] and that the warring creeds of liberalism, communism, and even "institutional" Christianity are all imperfect and incomplete.[17] Others, however, particularly among the earliest nuclear pacifists, hold a more traditional dark picture of communism.[18]

A more common theme of nuclear pacifists is that the struggle against communism should not be viewed primarily in military terms. The authors of A Christian Approach to Nuclear War disclaim any notion that Christianity can be defended by exterminating communists. Instead they plead with their fellow Christians "to help in carrying out our primary Christian task of winning adherents of Communism to Christ by the preaching of the Gospel and the daily practice of the ministry of reconciliation which he has entrusted to us."[19] Stein points out the ideological, social, and

---

[16]Stein, NWCC, pp. 39-40.

[17]Stein, Peace on Earth, pp. 269-271.

[18]E.g., E. I. Watkin, "Unjustifiable War," in Morals and Missiles, ed. Charles Thompson (London, 1959). Hereafter cited as Watkin, "Unjustifiable War".

[19]Christian Approach, p. 12.

economic nature of the contest:

> It is, moreover, self-evident that no military
> means at all can shield us against communism as an
> ideological force. Ideologically, communism is an
> infection that can only be arrested by better health.
> Military strength is as irrelevant from this point of
> view as it is to the destruction of cancer. Even
> a defeat of Russia and China might actually be fol-
> lowed by a resurgence of communism throughout the
> world. The enormous sums spent on nuclear armaments
> might be used more effectively to combat communism
> by a world-wide campaign against poverty and the
> evils that make the communist solution attractive.[20]

The corollary to the idea that communist ideology cannot be defeated

militarily is that neither can Western and Christian values, but I will

deal with that theme in the section "Hope and History" in the next chapter.

A second corollary which I want to mention here is that an immoral military

posture is itself a threat to the values it is supposed to defend. As

R. A. Markus says,

> We are being, increasingly, swept along the current
> towards accepting war as a master, with a dynamism
> of its own, to which our standards of right and
> wrong are not applicable, a process which enslaves
> those who participate in it and subdues them to its
> purposes, much in the same way as does a totalitarian
> state.[21]

Donald Bloesch points out that not only moral but also spiritual and

political values are threatened by the "cold war." The cold war fosters

"a growing pathological obsession" with our own security, and locates that

security in our nuclear stockpile rather than in God.[22] In addition, "It

---

[20]Stein, NWCC, p. 21.

[21] Markus, "Conscience", p. 87.

[22] Donald Bloesch, "The Christian and the Drift Towards War," Theology and Life , II (1959), 325. Hereafter cited as Bloesch, "The Christian".

might very well precipitate a situation in which the people will volun-
tarily surrender their integrity and freedom to an all-powerful state in
the interest of national security."[23] Thus according to nuclear pacifists
the mere political independence of Western societies is not enough to
maintain the values thought to be embodied in those societies. It is
equally important that the means of military defense be subordinated to
those values.

So far I have described the general debate about the respective consequences of nuclear pacifism and the continued reliance on nuclear weapons.
Now I would like to deal briefly with a particular aspect of that debate,
the consequences of a "bluff" position. J. Bryan Hehir is interesting in
this regard because he adopts such a position precisely on consequential
grounds.

In The New Nuclear Debate (New York, 1976), Hehir adopts a position
of nuclear pacifism regarding the use of nuclear weapons (pp. 47-50), but
he believes there is a need for a nuclear deterrent "to prevent the outbreak of conflict" (p. 52). On ethical grounds he would prefer to structure the deterrent along the counterforce lines suggested by Ramsey, but
"the strategic logic of deterrence in the post-MIRV era" (p. 57) prevents
him from now wanting to switch from a policy of mutual assured destruction
to a counterforce policy:

> Is it possible to ignore the latent consequences
> of moving away from the precarious stability of
> MAD; those consequences being precisely the fac-
> tors of risk or [read of?] misperception, miscal-
> culation, and the thrust toward first-strike
> policies which seem to accompany more accuracy

---

[23]Ibid.

> in weaponry or any indication that we are
> seeking to target an opponent's striking force.
> (Pp. 67-68)

Therefore on consequential grounds Hehir supports the MAD deterrence policy while maintaining that nuclear weapons may never be used (pp. 51-52).

Nuclear pacifists have little reason to debate the respective consequences of MAD or counterforce deterrence, since they reject any nuclear deterrence. And of course, my sources predate the debate of the 1970's and 1980's about switching from mutual assured destruction to counterforce deterrence (though following Secretary McNamara's speech of June, 1962, there was a similar debate, which nuclear pacifists largely ignored). However, nuclear pacifists do make the claim that there are unfavorable consequences of supporting a MAD "bluff" position.

First of all, say nuclear pacifists, any deterrence policy maintains the risk of nuclear war and may even provoke such a war. Secondly, there is not sufficient control of military forces to ensure that there will be no use of nuclear weapons even if the authorities so wished. Thirdly, maintaining a deterrent affirms the utility of nuclear weapons and therefore encourages their proliferation to other countries. All of these points are made in <u>A</u> <u>Christian</u> <u>Approach</u> <u>to</u> <u>Nuclear</u> <u>War</u>:

> Weapons which may be intended to deter also
> create suspicion and fear, and therefore
> inevitably provoke. Moreover, the contin-
> uance of the arms race daily heightens the
> risk that through accident or otherwise the
> precarious 'balance of terror' will collapse
> into war. Those who advance the formula that
> we should have weapons which we may under no
> circumstances use cannot entertain a reason-
> able hope that the determination to use is in
> their control, or even in the control of the
> central civil and military agencies of their

> government, since the decision may actually be
> made by a bomber pilot, a submarine commander
> or other subaltern or may actually be the result
> of a defect in a calculating machine. This
> approach amounts, therefore, to advocating a mis-
> leading gesture. It also leaves the way open for
> the acquisition of nuclear capability by more
> nations.[24]

Finally, nuclear pacifists maintain, as I noted in the discussion of

Ramsey's type D deterrence, that the "bluff" position is self-defeating:

a decision never to retaliate with nuclear weapons could not be made firm

without undermining the deterrent threat. While previously I focused on

the issue of the actual murderous intention of citizens, military personnel,

and political leaders, in this case the issue is whether restraint could

actually be exercised in a crisis. Norman Gottwald asks, "But if all-out

destruction as a threat has been the cornerstone of Western defense policies,

will the West possess sufficient moral restraint to withhold the use of

nuclear weapons under provocation?"[25]

---

[24] Christian Approach, pp. 5-6.

[25] Gottwald, "NR or NP?," p. 896. Cf. also Christian Approach, p. 6.

The Nature of Ethical Reasoning

To this point I have described the debate about the respective consequences of various policies in regard to nuclear weapons. That discussion raises a question about the nature of ethical reasoning: what is the
significance of the expected consequences of an action in morally evaluating that action? For the purposes of this study it will be sufficient
to answer that question initially on the basis of a simple distinction
between two basic types of ethical reasoning, teleology and deontology.
In teleological ethics every action is to be evaluated according to whether
it produces more good or more evil results, while deontological ethics
identifies certain actions that must be done or may not be done no matter
what consequences are likely to follow. When ethical methodology is
explicitly discussed in the nuclear debate, it is usually put in these
terms.

Some moralists and strategic thinkers, whom I will call consequentialists, adopt the teleological mode of thinking and believe that various
policies must be judged according to the results they are calculated to
produce. Ernest W. Lefever provides a clear example of this in his criticism of an article by the Christian statesman George F. Kennan. In 1959
Kennan said: "I can testify from personal experience that not only can
one never know, when one takes a far-reaching decision in foreign policy,
precisely what the consequences are going to be, but almost never do these
consequences fully coincide with what one intended or expected."[26] He

---

[26]George F. Kennan, "Foreign Policy and Christian Conscience,"
Atlantic Monthly, CCIII (1959); in The Moral Dilemma of Nuclear Weapons,
ed. William Clancy (New York, 1961), p. 69. Kennan is the father of the
"containment" policy toward the Soviet Union and probably the most prominent
living analyst of U.S. foreign policy. He is still a strong proponent of
multilateral nuclear disarmament.

said that statesmen should be guided by principle as well as by calculation, and on the basis of the principle of discrimination he repudiated
the use of nuclear weapons (though he did not call for unilateral disarmament).[27] Kennan also condemned the testing of atomic weapons. Lefever
complains that on these points Kennan has fallen into "legalism" and
"moral absolutism". Furthermore, "Mr. Kennan understands the limits of
human calculation in politics, but he fails to recognize its possibilities
...calculation is the life blood of politics and the heart of ethics.
Calculation is the bridge between the given and the desired, between
facts and dreams."[28]

In contrast to the consequentialists, most just war theorists hold
that such calculation can occur only within the limits of deontological
moral principles. Elizabeth Anscombe cites murder, adultery, and apostasy
as examples of prohibited actions: "These absolute prohibitions of
Christianity by no means exhaust its ethic; there is a large area where
what is just is determined partly by a prudent weighing up of consequences.
But the prohibitions are bedrock, and without them the Christian ethic
goes to pieces."[29] Along the same lines Paul Ramsey criticizes Lefever's
statement that calculation is the heart of ethics: "Far from this being
the case, we must affirm to the contrary that a wholly teleological view
of ethics amounts to the suspension of ethics."[30] For "...calculation is

---

[27]Ibid., pp. 75-76.

[28]Ernest W. Lefever, "Facts, Calculation and Political Ethics," in
The Moral Dilemma of Nuclear Weapons (New York, 1961), p. 38.

[29]G. E. M. Anscombe, "War and Murder," in Stein, NWCC, pp. 57-58.
Hereafter cited as Anscombe, "War and Murder".

[30]Paul Ramsey, "Right and Wrong Calculation," in The Moral Dilemma
of Nuclear Weapons (New York, 1961), p. 48.

always only a subordinate part of moral judgment and to be entered upon logically only after the ethical guidelines of action have been fixed."[31] In the case of war, the issue is the prohibition of murder, as defined by the principles of discrimination and double effect.

Walter Stein is concerned to defend the deontological form of moral commitment as much as the nuclear pacifist conclusion. He makes it clear in his introduction to Nuclear Weapons and Christian Conscience that the nuclear pacifism advocated by the authors is not based on prudential grounds, for though nuclear weapons cannot provide security, neither can non-violent resistance in view of past communist actions. Rather, nuclear pacifism is urged on moral grounds, for "some things are intolerable, irrespective of circumstances," and among them are the "total war" which nuclear deterrence threatens.[32] Also, in Peace on Earth Stein criticizes the common assumption that there are no absolute moral limits governing international behavior. According to Stein this has resulted not only in a moral but in a practical crisis (p. 48): the self-interested pursuit of national-ideological goals remains unchecked even though in a nuclear age it conflicts with the goal of national physical survival (pp. 46-47). Thus "The most basic political task of the peace movement is to liberate foreign politics--and all who profess that peace is their profession--from their apocalyptic pragmatism" (p. 49, author's italics). Therefore Stein criticizes "unilateralism as a theory of disarmament procedure" rather than as "the expression of an absolute commitment" (p. 50, author's italics): "one cannot cast out pragmatism by pragmatism" (p. 59).

---

[31]Ibid., p. 51.
[32]Stein, NWCC, p. 23.

In short, for these just war theorists, politics, prudence, and charity operate within the limits of moral absolutes. Not even the right of self-defense can overrule the principle of discrimination. Of course, nuclear pacifists and counterforce theorists disagree on whether a nuclear war could be fought without violating the rights of the innocent, but their common ethical approach does not allow any consequentialist calculus to violate those rights. Similarly rejected is any justification for doing "the lesser of two evils", if evil is defined as moral evil. In deontological ethics one may be driven to do tragic acts but not to do inherently · evil acts, or, to put it another way, one may never adopt evil means to achieve good ends.[33]

A deontological commitment to (in this case) the principle of discrimination does not necessarily mean that just war thinkers admit that their policies would be found wanting on consequentialist grounds. For instance, Paul Ramsey states that when it comes to acts of indiscriminate bombing or the all-out use of megaton weapons, "it is better to suffer evil than to do it,"[34] and Christians must have nothing to do with such actions even if Christianity should have to become a sect.[35] At the same time, however, Ramsey never admits that military/political prudence conflicts with moral absolutes, even when his view of prudent policy changes somewhat. Thus in War and the Christian Conscience when he held that only counterforce

---

[33] Cf. L. L. McReavy, "The Morality of Nuclear Warfare," The Tablet, CCXI, p. 292; Stein, Peace on Earth, pp. 38, 267; Anscombe, "War and Murder," P. 59.

[34] Ramsey, WCC, p. 199.

[35] Ibid., p. 270.

deterrence could be moral, he also held that only counterforce deterrence could be effective. Later, when it seemed that a counter-city deterrent threat might be necessary, he suggested a "bluff" position to allow it some moral legitimacy. When in 1972 he again held that a "bluff" was untenable, he also stated that a MAD posture was "not a good idea in the first place."[36] Thus for Ramsey a decision between prudence and absolute moral principle was never necessary.

Nuclear pacifists are generally more willing, if still reluctant, to admit that their adherence to moral absolutes could result in unhappy consequences, at least in the short run. Norman Gottwald, for example, says that even in the face of a communist threat "the Christian nuclear pacifist is prepared to accept the worst possible consequence of unilateral nuclear disarmament."[37] At the same time, nuclear pacifists express their faith that in the long run or in terms of God's redemptive activity their policy would produce more good than capitulation to the apparent expediency of the moment. Thus when it is pushed to its foundations in ultimate hope the teleological/deontological distinction breaks down.[38]

Even on a less ultimate level, this dichotomy is inadequate to locate some of the ethical approaches employed in the nuclear debate. Therefore I will briefly discuss some of the variations from the pattern I have described.

---

[36]Paul Ramsey, "The MAD Nuclear Policy," Worldview, XV (1972), 18. Ramsey does not elaborate why it is not a good idea, but his thinking probably returns to that of War and the Christian Conscience.

[37]Gottwald, "NR or NP?," p. 898.

[38]One who has criticized such categorization is John Howard Yoder, "Radical Reformation Ethics in Ecumenical Perspective," Journal of Ecumenical Studies, XV (1978), 647-661.

In discussing the principle of discrimination, the philosopher and lawyer Richard Wasserstrom notes[39] that it may be held in three ways: 1) The direct killing of the innocent is absolutely immoral regardless of the circumstances. 2) It is prima facie immoral: in special overriding circumstances it may be done but even then it involves some measure of immorality. 3) It is typically wrong but when justified by the circumstances there is nothing immoral about it. (Pp. 98-99) The first position Wasserstrom calls "absolutist" and I have called "deontological"; he (correctly) identifies Elizabeth Anscombe and John C. Ford as "absolutist". The third view is a pure form of what I have above called "consequentialism". In theory Wasserstrom rejects the absolutist view because it does not take sufficient account of the consequences of actions (p. 99), and instead he adopts the second position (p. 100). However, in practice he comes to a nuclear pacifist stance because the killing of great numbers of innocent persons is such a central feature of modern war, particularly nuclear war, that no major war could come close to meeting the heavy burden of proof required to justify the intentional killing of the innocent (pp. 100-101).

Donald Bloesch is another nuclear pacifist who falls roughly in Wasserstrom's second category. Following the reasoning of Reinhold Niebuhr, he says that it is sinful to engage in war but it is also sinful to abstain from it. In the present age no alternative is free from sin; war is always evil but it may be the lesser of several evils.[40] Apparently, however,

---

[39] Richard Wasserstrom, "On the Morality of War: A Preliminary Inquiry," Stanford Law Review, XXI (1969), 1627-1656. Portions reprinted in War and Morality, ed. Richard Wasserstrom (Belmont, California, 1970), pp. 78-101. Page references will be to War and Morality.

[40] Bloesch, "The Christian," pp. 320-321.

Bloesch believes that nuclear war is so evil that it can never be the lesser evil.[41] Thus Bloesch disagrees greatly with deontological nuclear pacifists on methodological grounds but he comes to the same conclusion. While Bloesch and Wasserstrom are not full consequentialists, their methods allow more room for consequential considerations, and thus presumably for the arguments of strategic and political analysis, than does deontological nuclear pacifism.

One author who does not fit either the dichotomy I offered or the three categories Wasserstrom describes is J. Bryan Hehir. As I noted previously, Hehir adopts a "bluff" position on deterrence, even though he says that "by tradition and training I have been shaped by a deontological style of moral analysis."[42] In effect he adopts a deontological approach to any fight-the-war policy and a teleological approach to a deter-the-war policy. Hehir attempts to do this by separating from the deterrent threat any actual intention to use nuclear weapons. Nuclear pacifists are not alone in denying that this can be done. Michael Walzer, who has constructed a full just war theory, admits that in deterrence "we intend the killings under certain circumstances."[43] He thus fits into Wasserstrom's second category of allowing an action which is required by the circumstances but which remains morally tainted. Walzer differs from

---

[41]Ibid., p. 322.

[42]Gessert and Hehir, NND, p. 66.

[43]Michael Walzer, Just and Unjust Wars: A Moral Argument with Historical Illustrations (New York, 1977), p. 272.

[44]Ibid., pp. 282-283.

from Bloesch in that he considers that only in certain cases of grave necessity, such as that presented by the nuclear threat, is one allowed or inherently required to engage in evil actions.

A writer who explicitly rejects the deontology/teleology dichotomy is the strategic analyst Robert A. Gessert. He says that he is attracted to consequentialist reasoning but is disturbed that some, like Hehir, use it to justify mutual assured destruction deterrence, whereas he advocates counterforce deterrence. In the end he describes his position as "covenantal" ethics: the United States has committed itself in the North Atlantic Treaty and the Non-Proliferation Treaty to use its strategic deterrent to protect other nations.[45] Another term for this might be "responsibility" ethics and no doubt many writers on the subject could be described in this way. It is useful in reminding us of the actual political context of the nuclear debate, for "consequentialism" can be thought of very abstractly. Nevertheless this position too could be pressed with the question, are there some things that ought never to be done? As we have seen, most of the just war theorists in my sample would answer, "Yes: the direct killing of the innocent ought never to be done."

---

[45]Robert Gessert, "Deterrence and the Defense of Europe," in Ford and Winters, ENS?, pp. 107-111.

Proof and Competence

The fact that most of the moralists in my sample agree on particular moral norms, the principles of proportionality and discrimination, and on the deontological logic with which the latter should be applied, does not of course assure that they came to the same conclusions about modern war. One of the most important differences between nuclear pacifists and counterforce advocates is that they have different assumptions about where the burden of proof lies in the issue. L. L. McReavy illustrates the counterforce side when he rejects nuclear pacifism because it is possible, even though highly unlikely, that nuclear weapons could be justly used in a war of self-defense. Therefore final judgment must be reserved until war actually breaks out.[46] R. A. Markus admits that it is true as a "marginal theoretical possibility" that there could be justifiable nuclear war. On such a basis a Catholic might defend his manufacturing and marketing of contraceptives on the ground that possibly people will buy them in order to melt them down to make rubber balls for their children to play with.[47] According to Markus certainty cannot be obtained in ethical matters and to ignore the nature of nuclear weapons and the very likely consequences of their use "is at best moral blindness, at worst hypocritical self-excuse."[48] As I noted in Chapter II, most nuclear pacifists consider it immoral even to risk nuclear holocaust; thus they place the burden of proof

---

[46]L. L. McReavy, "The Debate on the Morality of Future War," Clergy Review, VL (1960), 87. Hereafter cited as McReavy, "Debate."

[47]Markus, "Conscience," pp. 69-70.

[48]Ibid., p. 70.

on those who would justify rather than on those who would condemn the possession of nuclear weapons.

These two different conceptions of where the burden of proof lies result in different ideas about the role of findings of fact in the argument. This is most evident in the dialogue about deterrence between Walter Stein and Paul Ramsey in Peace, the Churches and the Bomb and in "Again, the Justice of Deterrence" (Ramsey, Just War, pp. 314-366). Both agree that a finding of fact is central to Stein's argument. They disagree radically on whether that is an asset or a liability. Stein believes that by quoting military and political leaders he has proven the actual facts which demonstrate that present deterrence policy is based on murderous intention and thus must be condemned (pp. 20-23, 76). Ramsey disputes this finding a bit, but more importantly he says that Stein must not only establish his case with regard to the present but must show that "the fact-situation he describes is necessarily and unchangeably true" (p. 43, author's italics). He goes on to discuss deterrent effects of types B, C, and D to show that there could be an effective deterrent that did not depend upon murderous intention (see Chapter III above).

Ramsey thus claims that nuclear pacifists must show that not only is present deterrence policy immoral but any nuclear deterrence would have to be immoral before they can demand of governments unilateral nuclear disarmament. At the same time he denies that moralists or church bodies are qualified to make the findings of fact such proof requires; their competence is only to speak in moral terms on the moral issues involved (p. 44). To put it in simple terms, according to Ramsey moralists can only make "if, then" statements; it is up to citizens and officials to judge the truth of the "if" (p. 44; Just War, p. 339). Ramsey has thus posited

a distinction between the moralist _qua_ moralist and the moralist as
citizen, and made it impossible in principle for a moralist _qua_ moralist
to be a nuclear pacifist. In the face of this Stein can only reiterate
his facts (p. 76), lament that Ramsey has failed to challenge them
(p. 77), and complain that Ramsey has apparently left no room for reasoned
discussion (p. 75).[49]

In summary, embedded in the nuclear weapons debate are various issues
of political judgment and ethical methodology. While their critics focus
on the disastrous consequences which they believe would follow unilateral
nuclear disarmament, nuclear pacifists believe that a good case can be
made for their position on consequentialist grounds. The argument about
the results of various policies in turn depends upon an analysis of the
nature of the conflict between East and West. At the same time, the
nuclear weapons debate is not only about consequences but also about the
nature of ethical reasoning. Here most just war theorists are united in
holding that the principle of discrimination is a deontological norm which
must be maintained despite the consequences. However, nuclear pacifists
and counterforce theorists differ in their ideas about where the burden
of proof lies in deciding whether nuclear weapons must be totally condemned. While all of these matters make the discussion complex enough,
important theological issues are involved as well, and it is to them that
I will turn in the next chapter.

---

[49]Stein (p. 75) quotes Ramsey's statement that moral judgment is within but factual determination is without the competence of a church council.
Though he labels this statement as definitive of the obvious, Stein apparently disagrees only with the first half of the statement, since he questions why it is so obvious that "a responsible body of judges" cannot judge
these facts. Ramsey correctly notes that Stein's statement is unclear (_Just
War_, p. 337). I will deal with this issue further in Chapter VI.

Chapter V

THE JUST WAR TRADITION, CHRISTIAN HOPE, AND THE CHURCH

Hope and History

Political and ethical issues can never be separated from questions
of theological and philosophical commitment. This is especially true of
the nuclear debate which is sometimes cast in terms of two basic alternatives, "red" or dead. Such stark language presses the argument to
questions of the nature of hope within and beyond history, and we begin
this chapter by exploring the various views of hope and history.

Nuclear pacifists are shocked that mankind now has the power to end
human history, a right which they believe belongs to God alone and should
be exercised only by Him.[1] They exhibit a sense of urgency that the
nuclear threat be faced immediately. Nevertheless most nuclear pacifists
have hope that mankind as created or redeemed has the resources to avert
catastrophe. As Stein says, there is not much time to say "No", but men
"can say 'No' to the feverish, blood-sick self-destructiveness of the
nuclear terror."[2] A Christian Approach to Nuclear War expresses it in
terms of Christian redemption: "God has not called us to be dragged like
slaves in the wake of history plunging to its doom but to be messengers
and servants of Christ who is the Lord of history and the victor over the

---

[1]Christian Approach, p. 9; Gottwald, "NR or NP?," p. 896.
[2]Stein, Peace on Earth, p. 289.

128

demonic forces in it" (p. 12). Sin is subtle and powerful, but to blame our poor ethical performance on an inability to do otherwise would be to "mock the Incarnation, deny the Atonement, and flout the ethical mandates of the New Testament" (p. 9).

As I pointed out in the previous chapter, nuclear pacifists hope that the policies and attitudes they recommend will have salutary political effects. Nevertheless they face even the prospect of communist domination with hope, not simply because human life would survive but because "the survival of life under tyranny could be creative, being deliberately chosen in consonance with Christian faith and hope".[3] There would be suffering, certainly--but it would be meaningful suffering.[4]

E. I. Watkin, in his article "Unjustifiable War" chides for their lack of faith those Catholics who believe that communism is so evil that any means, including immoral atomic warfare, may be used to fight it. This view unconsciously surrenders to the belief of Marxist materialism that material force is more powerful and thus more real than spiritual force, for it admits that "the sword of atomic weapons can decisively and finally defeat the sword of the spirit" (p. 54). According to Watkin such a view calls into question the belief that the ultimate reality is God, who is spirit (p. 54). These Christians have little faith in God's action, for:

> They cannot believe that, if in obedience
> to His law they refuse to resist Communist
> aggression by flagrantly immoral means, by
> wholesale massacre and mutilation of the

---

[3] Christian Approach, p. 10.

[4] Ibid.; Stein, NWCC, p. 41.

> innocent, and even if He should permit the
> Communists to conquer the world, He can or
> will enable His servants to win by spiritual
> weapons victory over a materially triumphant
> foe. The historic victory of the Cross, though
> the centre of their religion, seems to them
> irrelevant to the realities of the contemporary
> situation, something which cannot be continued,
> in a sense repeated, today. They cannot be
> persuaded that the victory of faith, which
> overcomes the world, can overcome the Communist
> world. (p. 55)

Watkin suggests that God is calling us in the present moment to defeat all forms of materialism by rejecting immoral methods of warfare as "a supreme act of faith in His Omnipotence" (p. 55). However, this is not simply blind faith, for there is evidence that despite official atheism there is passionate interest in Russia in the question of whether God exists. In fact, "There may well be more genuine religion in Russia today than in Scandinavia, possibly even in Britain" (p. 56). The freedom and aspiration of the human spirit to find God has proven too deep to be suppressed by Marxism. If this is true in Russia, it would be even more the case in countries with a tradition of political freedom.

From this discussion it is evident that for Watkin the "defeat" of communist materialism, at least in the short run, does not depend upon preserving the national sovereignty or political institutions of the West. Even the institutional integrity of the Church is not an issue. What is crucial is the religious quest for God. Other Christian nuclear pacifists too, when it comes to matters of ultimate commitment, place more value in moral law, religion, and the Church than in military necessity, political values, and the nation. They do not specify, however, just what they would hope for in a world dominated by communist governments. Elizabeth Anscombe says that instead of a vague hope of "the spirit" triumphing over force, Christians have a definite faith in the divine promises that the church cannot fail.[5] At the end of <u>Nuclear</u> <u>Weapons</u> <u>and</u> <u>Christian</u> <u>Conscience</u> Walter Stein acknowledges that unilateral disarmament, which "could hardly fail to result in a communist domination" (p. 150), and other steps toward peace, involve great dangers.

> But the more the Church stands to lose, humanly
> speaking, by committing herself, and her mission,
> to these dangers, the more clearly her existence
> will be seen as a divine fact. The future may then
> safely be left to God. Pharaoh's armies may be
> close upon us and the Sea extend before our feet,
> but we know that our Redeemer liveth. (p. 151)

The "future" is unspecified in Stein's statement. Implicit and occasionally explicit throughout the writings of Christian nuclear pacifists is a hope not only within but beyond history, for God is the author of history and Christ is its Lord. Behind the moral and political issues stand the reality of Heaven and Hell.[6]

It is thus on the basis of their hope (and fear) that nuclear pacifists are enabled to take a radical moral stand. Counterforce theorists do not disagree with the ultimate hope of salvation, but they place their penultimate hopes on creating the possibility of limited nuclear war rather than on the renunciation of nuclear weapons. Thus John Courtney Murray urges work on many levels of policy formation, including public education: "To say that the possibility of limited war cannot be created

---

[5]Anscombe, "War and Murder," p. 61.

[6]Elizabeth Anscombe for one is quite explicit that we ought to fear God more than the Russians, for only He can destroy the unrepentant disobedient in hell. Anscombe, "War and Murder," pp. 61-62.

by intelligence and energy, under the direction of a moral imperative, is to succumb to some sort of determinism in human affairs."[7] The Catholic strategist and public servant Thomas E. Murray similarly says that "A nuclear war can still be a limited war. To believe otherwise is to deny that man is a rational being capable of controlling his own actions."[8] Even the enemy must be presumed rational, as Paul Ramsey says.[9] Thus both nuclear pacifists and counterforce theorists express faith in the rationality and morality of mankind, but they hope for different responses to the nuclear dilemma.

A few Christian theologians attack the hope with which nuclear pacifists face the possibility of communist domination. For example, Rev. Robert Mohan, S.S., seems to believe that while nothing can deprive us of eternal salvation, the Church can be destroyed in countries controlled by Soviet communism.

Thus in his article "Thermonuclear War and the Christian"[10] Mohan says that "the lasting city to which we are destined cannot be destroyed by the folly of men" (p. 77), but he also says that:

---

[7] Murray, MMW, p. 18.

[8] Thomas E. Murray, "Morality and Security: The Forgotten Equation," Morality and Modern Warfare, ed. William Nagle (Baltimore, 1960), p. 63.

[9] Ramsey, Just War, p. 357.

[10] Robert Paul Mohan, "Thermonuclear War and the Christian," in Christian Ethics and Nuclear Warfare, eds. Ubrich Allers and William V. O'Brien (Washington, D.C., 1961), pp. 66-78. Page references are to this article.

> We would all do well to forget the romantic
> notions of a Church of Silence, heroically admin-
> istering the sacraments behind the iron and bam-
> boo curtains. It is closer to the truth to recognize
> the brutal facts that the Church, its priests, and
> its catechists have been systematically and effic-
> iently exterminated in lands where communism has
> triumphed--even if it is tactically advisable for
> the Soviets to make concessions, as they do in
> Poland. I do not consider such a land, however
> intact its buildings, as preferable to widespread
> destruction. (p. 76)

In regard to the idea that we should remember the Providence of God,

Mohan says that Providence includes "the natural power that is given to

men to contribute to their destiny. It is God's will that we be partici-

pants, not mere spectators, in the great drama of history" (p. 76).

Harold O. J. Brown is a conservative Protestant theologian who also

believes that Western religious and political values are totally incom-

patible with communism. He is willing to risk the annihilation of the

United States in order to resist enslavement by totalitarian communism.

Because of their hope of salvation beyond this world, Christians are pre-

pared for the risk:

> Christians, unlike secularists, have the
> great consolation that they can try conscien-
> tiously to do their best without being in a
> panic about the outcome--which is after all in
> the hands of God, who will save all who trust
> in Christ, war or no war. In one way, perhaps
> it is the Christians who are the free world's
> hope of remaining free, for it is we alone who
> can dare to risk losing much or all in war to
> forestall what we consider a still greater evil,
> the world domination of a totalitarian, atheistic
> system as pictured by George Orwell in Nineteen
> Eighty-Four.[11]

---

[11] Harold Brown (with Lewis Smedes, et al.), "Rumors of Wars,"
Eternity, June, 1980, p. 17.

Brown believes that at some point military action will be necessary against the Soviets, so "it is important to have at least some Christians in positions of authority, people who will not be 'kept in bondage by the fear of death,' as Hebrews puts it".[12]

While he would certainly reject Brown's crusading spirit, Paul Ramsey does share some of Brown's perspective. And while, like Brown, he is not refuting religious nuclear pacifists, it is worthwhile to note the kind of arguments he makes on the basis of Christian hope. In Chapter 9 of War and the Christian Conscience (pp. 192-209) Dr. Ramsey refutes the thesis of Philip Toynbee and others that it is better to immediately negotiate with the Soviet Union from a position of weakness than to continue to risk nuclear annihilation.[13] First Ramsey says that we always knew the world would end, and knowledge of an end by nuclear destruction in twenty-four hours has no more inherent power to render present life meaningless than does an end for natural cosmic reasons two billion years from now (p. 193). Secondly, while he agrees that by prudential calculation there can be no proportionate reason to choose to destroy mankind (p. 200), this is very different from risking such destruction (pp. 195, 198). Liberty (p. 198) and justice (pp. 205-206) can only be preserved by force, which today can be used only at the risk of vastly destructive nuclear war. All must undertake this risk for, says Ramsey, "On their way to the Heavenly City the children of God make use of the pax-ordo of the earthly city and acknowledge their share in responsibility for its preser-

---

[12] Ibid.

[13] Philip Toynbee, ed., The Fearful Choice: A Debate on Nuclear Policy (Detroit, 1959).

vation" (p. 205). Ramsey agrees with the conclusion of the Calhoun Commission report, Atomic Warfare and the Christian Faith, that what Christians in particular bring to the situation is hope in both historical and trans-historical terms: historical in that even after nuclear war there might be survivors in remote places of whom God would make great peoples; trans-historical in that God will hold His children in His eternal presence (pp. 208-209).

Thus Ramsey says that because of their hope in the "Heavenly City" Christians need not adopt a nuclear pacifism based on fear of death in a nuclear holocaust. Elsewhere[14] he says that it is because our secular-ized age no longer believes in the supernatural life that the sacredness of the individual is misconceived and politics is improperly spiritual-ized as not requiring force. Only when earthly life and politics are placed in proper perspective are individuals willing to sacrifice their lives and political communities willing to use force to achieve limited and precarious political goods. At the same time, only such a perspective on the limited nature of earthly life can keep war limited once it actually breaks out, for Americans convert their grand goals prior to war into grand goals to be accomplished by war, and unlimited goals lead to the use of unlimited force.[15]

---

[14] Ramsey, Just War, pp. 14-18.

[15] This is a central theme of Ramsey's article, "What Americans Ordinarily Think about Justice in War," in Just War, pp. 42-69.

The Just War Tradition: Universal and Particular

According to Paul Ramsey then it is their religious hope which
enables Christians to risk nuclear war in the service of justice. For
Christian nuclear pacifists it is their religious hope which enables them
to denounce nuclear war as required by justice. Despite their sharp
differences both parties rely on Christian hope as they employ the just
war criteria in politics. Thus it might appear that the just war tradition can only be useful to Christians. However, counterforce advocates
and nuclear pacifists agree that the just war criteria both belong to a
particular tradition and have universal validity for all people. Or, to
be more exact, both groups assume the universality of the just war
criteria but also locate them in a particular tradition which may be
variously defined in different contexts.

One form of particularity assumed by the authors in my sample is
that the just war tradition is a Roman Catholic moral tradition. Thus
they show a great deal of interest in the statements of modern popes and
bishops, the Second Vatican Council, Catholic theologians, and other
Catholic writers. At other times these writers consider the just war
criteria to form a Christian tradition, and they refer to the history of
Christian thought on the problem of war and to the recent statements of
Christian groups and individuals. They may also appeal to the Christian
conscience. More broadly, reference may be made to the Judeo-Christian
tradition, and the Hebrew and Christian Scriptures are cited as sources
of divine commands and theological concepts. In geographical/political/
cultural rather than religious terms, just war thought is claimed as a
Western tradition.

In these various ways the authors in my sample locate the just war theory in particular communities and traditions. At the same time they consider it to be a universal ethic grounded in natural law. They may affirm the just war norms by appeals to human conscience, reason, common sense, or simply political prudence. Nuclear pacifists especially tend to claim that to hold their position is simply to assert one's own humanity[16] and to recognize "the human family" as a unity.[17]

Those writers who take note of the question of how the just war tradition may be conceived of as universal and particular at the same time usually claim that the particular tradition only makes more explicit or more insistent what should be obvious on other grounds. Thus Elizabeth Anscombe says that the immorality of killing the innocent is so obvious that only the strength of human pride and malice required it to be promulgated by Moses and the prophets, and only the fading of Christianity from the mind of the West make it now seem to be too intransigent of a demand.[18] Walter Stein, too, after quoting British and American deterrent threats of assured destruction says:

> One does not need to be a Christian--nor indeed any sort of theist at all--to recognize in these threats a deracination from the humanity within ourselves. But we have the Prophets and the Gospels; and we have a full and precise tradition of the Church's thinking, evolved over the centuries, about the tolerable limits of war.[19]

---

[16]E.g., Markus, "Conscience," p. 87.

[17]Stein, Peace on Earth, p. 1, following Pacem in Terris.

[18]Anscombe, "War and Murder," pp. 55-56.

[19]Stein, NWCC, p. 31.

Almost by definition, the just war tradition admits no major differences between the precepts of the Old Testament, the New Testament, and natural law. Occasionally nuclear pacifists use the Cross as a symbol and model of suffering, but usually they do not suggest a difference between the Christian ethics and other forms of ethics. When L. L. McReavy did detect in the symposium <u>Morals and Missiles</u> (ed. Charles Thompson, London, 1959) a tendency to disparage natural law in favor of the imitation of Christ, he was quick to offer "the reminder that the natural law is no less divine in origin and authority than 'Christian ethics', and that it was neither changed nor augmented substantially by Christ."[20]

In theory then just war thinkers have at their disposal various approaches for addressing different audiences in just war categories. Some do maintain a predominantly general approach throughout their pieces.[21] Others, like Ramsey, often move back and forth between general and explicitly Christian terms. Most often, however, the writers in my sample dwell primarily on Christian tradition, authorities, and authors. This is partly a function of my selectivity and partly a function of the context in which they write. It also reflects the difficulty of arguing in two modes at once.

---

[20] McReavy, "Debate," p. 80.
[21] E.g. Markus, "Conscience".

The Role of the Church

According to these moralists the principles of the just war tradition are binding on all nations and individuals but reside in a special way in the Church. This raises the question of the role of the Church in a world full of nuclear weapons. Here there are some differences, so we must again separate nuclear pacifists from their critics.

I have noted previously that nuclear pacifists (among others) follow papal teaching in urging an atmosphere of international understanding and cooperation. Catholics at least point out that the Church as an institution transcending national and ideological differences can directly contribute to this goal.[22]

More often the Church is called to serve as a moral guide and political influence within Western societies. Francis Winters says that "as institutional representatives of the claims of conscience" churches should speak out more in trying to reshape American strategic policies.[23] Walter Stein too calls for Christian leaders to instruct the conscience of the nation and its political leaders, whether or not they are willing to listen to Christian imperatives.[24] He urges government support for unilateralism aided by a popular mandate, along with "missionary involvement" by academics in a serious search for remedies to international conflict and injustice.[25] As we have seen, nuclear pacifists have made

---

[22]Stein, in Peace on Earth, p. 59 sees the churches as playing a "key role" in East/West dialogue, but he does not specify that role. Lawler in Peace, Churches, Bomb, p. 36, suggests that the Church foster greater contacts between ministers of religion from the rival powers.

[23]Ford and Winters, ENS?, p. 46.

[24]Stein, Peace on Earth, pp. 39-40.

[25]Ibid., pp. 58-59.

various proposals, though I have not sought to record them fully. Finally, Markus urges people to transcend usual political allegiances to vote only for candidates who unconditionally reject nuclear weapons.[26]

Nuclear pacifists are not content to wait for a political solution to the problem of nuclear weapons. Just as they urge unilateral nuclear disarmament for nations (if necessary), so they urge unilateral nuclear "disarmament" for individuals and particularly Christian individuals. R. A. Markus admits that while it is mandatory to withdraw one's consent to waging war, since this will or might be done with immoral means, it is difficult to draw the line on which actions are prohibited.[27] Nevertheless it is clear that at a minimum one must refuse all military service.[28] Watkin says simply that Catholics who are convinced of the immorality of nuclear weapons cannot "employ, prepare or co-operate with such warfare."[29] Presumably this means at least that one cannot participate in the manufacture, transportation, or use of nuclear weapons.

Walter Stein raises but does not answer the question of whether a statesman recognizing the moral demands of unilateralism would be justified in remaining in office only if there were rapid progress toward international agreements, or whether only relative success compared to other candidates would be enough.[30] Francis Winters, however, is convinced

---

[26]Markus, "Conscience," p. 87. Markus has both Christians and non-Christians in mind. Stein holds out a little bit of hope for Britain's Labour Party to maintain a serious commitment to unilateralism. Stein, Peace on Earth, p. 51.

[27]Markus, "Conscience," pp. 82-83.

[28]Ibid., pp. 82, 84. Again, Markus claims that this action is necessary for all persons.

[29]Watkin, "Unjustifiable War," p. 62.

[30]Stein, Peace on Earth, p. 45.

that even the 1979 statement of Cardinal Krol,[31] which stops short of a full nuclear pacifism, places Catholic political and military officials in a dilemma: the Constitutional duties they have assumed by oath of office may require them to order or carry out a threatened or actual use of nuclear weapons, which the bishops have prohibited. They will have to choose between politics and religion, between the state and the church.[32]

Nuclear pacifists call for such actions not because they are required by political expediency but because they are required for bearing witness. Witness first, as Stein says, "simply to our humanity and obligations as men. There is no escape from this challenge. One rejects, or one accepts. One protests, or one condones."[33] But more is at stake, for as individual Christians we deny or affirm our Lord, and influence others who will judge our Faith by our faith. Finally, says Stein, pope, bishops, priests and laymen together form the collective witness of the (Roman Catholic) Church, making Christ's inherent presence in the Church harder or easier to see.

Such witness, say nuclear pacifists, is not to be confused with withdrawal or Pharisaical purity.[34] Perhaps the one who comes the closest to withdrawal is Donald Bloesch,[35] who seems to expect either a nuclear

---

31
    Cardinal John Krol, "SALT II: A Statement of Support," Origins, IX, 195-199.
32
    Francis Winters, "The Bow or the Cloud?," America, July 25, 1981, pp. 29-30.
33
    Stein, NWCC, p. 147. The rest of this paragraph is based on the same page.
34
    Stein, Peace on Earth, p. 59; Markus, "Conscience," p. 87.
35
    Bloesch, "The Christian". The rest of this paragraph is based on pp. 325-326. Bloesch denies that he is advocating withdrawal or isolation, p. 326.

war, a communist takeover, or the rise of dictatorship. He says that the church must disengage itself from the cold war and prepare for a world in chaos by establishing many more mission stations to carry the Evangel throughout the world "while there is still time". It must also establish hospitals and "lighthouses" in remote sections of the country as centers of spiritual life. If necessary the church "must go underground" to preserve the purity of its doctrine and way of life. It may have to bear witness to the Kingdom's "ultimate standard of sacrificial love and brotherhood" by suffering at the hands of foreign communists or American dictators who gain control of the country.

I have already mentioned in the section on hope that other nuclear pacifists too are prepared to accept suffering. As examples and sources of encouragement they turn to the Christian martyrs of past and present. As Walter Stein says in Peace on Earth, "The martyr, facing his witness, only knows: 'this is my call'; he cannot know whether his sacrifice will bear fruit among his neighbors" (p. 272). An example is Franz Jagerstatter, whose sacrifice has an incalculable posthumous power (p. 273). On the level of corporate witness, Stein points to the failure of the German Catholic Church to protest the Nazi wars, the silence of the Holy See on the "Final Solution", and the failure to protest Allied saturation and atomic bombing (p. 273). "In each of these cases, a forthright, witnessing denunciation of Satan's works could well have had decisive exorcising repercussions, either immediately or in the long run--history's and eternity's long run" (p. 274).

Thus according to Stein when protest is the only avenue open, it must be done even when it seems in human terms to be inexpedient, because "it participates in the divine expediency of redemption" (p. 279); it is the 'folly' of the Cross (p. 272). Yet in the present situation the world, caught in the inexpediency of its own nuclear expediency, might turn to unilateralism as providing a way out (pp. 271, 280). "In such circumstances," says Stein, "protest and politics, prophecy and expediency, become imperatively inextricable" (p. 280). Thus according to Christian nuclear pacifists, the commitment to a deontological ethic, the nature of hope, and the role of the church all lead to the same point: a Christian witness which in the face of nuclear weapons is simply a reassertion of humanity.

The Divided Church

Rhetorically and logically this should be the last word on the role
of the church, but practically it is not. The vision of a church united
in witness gives way to the fact and prospect of a church divided. If
this were not so, of course, there would be no need for a debate about
nuclear pacifism.

For Roman Catholic moralists, a central concern in such an important
matter must be the teaching of the Holy See. Early nuclear pacifists are
quick to point out Pope Pius XII's condemnation of total war, but they
usually admit that he never absolutely ruled out the use of nuclear
weapons in a defensive war.[36] E. I. Watkin in his article "Unjustifiable
War" offers various reasons for this: Only a small minority would obey
a papal condemnation of nuclear weapons and their preparation, dividing
the Catholic Church into two hostile camps (p. 60).[37] Governments would
persecute the obedient minority or all Catholics (p. 60). While Watkin
personally believes that just as the Cross led to victory so the crucifixion of the Church would lead to its moral redemption, the Pope could
not be sure of this, and at any rate Christ chose his own death alone,

---

[36] McReavy, "Debate," pp. 78-79, questions the "Catholic" nature of
Morals and Missiles because it does not take adequate account of the
magesterium. At the same time he admits that Pius XII never positively
approved of the use of nuclear weapons in self-defense, p. 85.

[37] William Wolff suggests that Rome announce that various sanctions
will follow the use of any atomic weapons: any individual involved will
be excommunicated; there will be seven days of penance (i.e. a general
strike) for all citizens following the use of nuclear weapons; governments
making first use of atomic weapons will be outlawed. While Wolff admits
that most Roman Catholics might not obey, government planners could not
be sure so they might be deterred. "The Church and the Bomb," America,
January 10, 1981, pp. 12-13.

while multitudes rely on the Pope (pp. 60-61). Many who did not follow but disobeyed him would be moved from a position of ignorant good faith to bad faith and thus formal sin (p. 61). And even we, says Watkin, who are moved in imagination by the crucifixion and resurrection of the Church may not be so ready to personally share in the crucifixion (p. 61). Finally, the Pope depends on the bureaucracy of the Papal Curia, "And the bureaucrat plays for safety. Not for him the risk, the venture of naked faith" (p. 61).

If for these reasons the Pope has not issued a command on the nuclear issue, still according to Watkin Catholics can find guidance in the canons of just war (p. 62). Others too argue that in this pressing issue it is wrong to simply wait for a definitive papal pronouncement;[38] sometimes this is accompanied by claims that the application of existent statements of the hierarchy should clearly lead to nuclear pacifist conclusions.[39] In general nuclear pacifists have more faith in the papacy than in local hierarchies, which have always been subject to captivity to nationalist feelings.[40] Stein says that since "Perhaps only the most solemn, authoritative pronouncement will suffice" to bring about an adequate Catholic witness on the subject of nuclear weapons, we should hope and pray for such a pronouncement.[41]

---

[38] Anscombe, "War and Murder," p. 52; Roger Smith, "The Witness of the Church," in Stein, NWCC, pp. 118-119.

[39] Stein, NWCC, p. 148.

[40] Watkin, "Unjustifiable War," pp. 57-58; P. J. Geech, "Conscience in Commission," in Stein, NWCC, pp. 93-94.

[41] Stein, NWCC, p. 148.

The opportunity for just such a statement arose at the Second Vatican Council. Theologians, political scientists and others debated Schema XIII and sometimes lobbied the bishops.[42] But in the end Walter Stein must lament that Vatican Council II failed to utter a radical "No" to nuclear violence. He can only wonder what such a call would have meant to Catholics, other Christians, those of other religions, and all people.[43]

One aspect of the divided Church is the fact that the critics of nuclear pacifism have their own opinions about the nature of the Church and its role in the nuclear debate. The whole thrust of John Courtney Murray's pamphlet Morality and Modern War is to offer the Catholic just war doctrine as a crucial element in the moral-political evaluation of war. Its primary value is "to set the right terms for rational debate on public policies" (p. 17), particularly by avoiding extreme alternatives by its insistence on the obligation of limited war (p. 18). Since it is a matter of "the public doctrine of the Church" (p. 5), presumably Catholics have a special obligation to advocate this theory, but Murray does not say so explicitly.

Paul Ramsey has a similar approach, though he hastens to add that the just war tradition is a Protestant as well as a Catholic heritage.[44] We noted previously his assertion that moralists can only illumine moral law

---

[42] James W. Douglass describes some of this activity in chapter 5 of his book The Non-Violent Cross: A Theology of Revolution and Peace (London, 1966), pp. 100-136.

[43] Stein, Peace on Earth, pp. 292-293.

[44] Ramsey, Just War, xi-xiv. Page references in the rest of the paragraph are to Just War.

while the determination of fact is left to government officials and
citizens. Similarly, churches should only expose the structures of
political reality (p. 20) and keep open as many options as are legitimate
(p. 19). According to Ramsey, religious communities as such are concerned
only with political doctrine, not the determination of policy, which is
the job of statesmen and citizens (pp. 19-20). Thus, "In politics the
church is only a theoretician" (p. 19, author's italics). "When the
churches turn their primary attention to trying to influence particular
policy decisions (to which they are tempted because every churchman is
also a citizen, and therefore a lesser magistrate), they do what they
ought not to have done" (p. 20). While Ramsey presses this point on
various fronts, it would certainly prohibit any official church body
from advocating unilateral disarmament except in extreme circumstances.

On the level of individual responsibility, counterforce advocates
like L. L. McReavy[45] say that it is not wrong to be in the armed services
or fight in war, but that one must refuse to cooperate with any immoral
military actions that might be undertaken in wartime.

Counterforce theorists are not impressed by calls to prophetic witness. While as I noted before most of them adopt a deontological stance
on the principle of discrimination, they see no present need for a radical
break with society. In fact, Ramsey concludes in this way his argument
that Pacem in terris is not an absolute modern-war pacifist document:
"I, at least, shall not believe that by Pacem in terris the Roman Catholic
Church became a 'sect' in relation to the military establishments of all

---

[45] McReavy, "Debate," p. 87.

nations...".[46]

Theodore Weber in _Peace, the Churches and the Bomb_ explores the ecclesiastical implications of nuclear pacifism:

> Throughout most of their history the Christian
> Churches have struggled with the problem of whether
> to seek influence as institutions in the world or to
> emphasize the marks of their differences from the
> world, whether to reach for power as an instrument
> of service in a history of infinite duration or to
> live a powerless existence as a community of the end-
> time. Roman Catholicism long ago decided predominantly
> although not exclusively, in favor of institutional
> influence. A strict and total moral rejection of
> nuclear armaments would call this decision into
> question. (P. 17)

Weber states that such a move would require Catholics to forego the use of power for the defense of self and the helpless neighbor and to withdraw from positions in government, military service, industry, research, and education which involve nuclear weapons (pp. 17-18). This would be a new form of witness and service, for the Church and the Christian "would be called rather to a genuinely eschatological existence in which they would trust solely in the grace and power of God" (p. 18).

Counterforce writers are anxious to avoid any such split between political power and morality, whether posed by nuclear pacifists or political "realists" who would not allow moral restraint to interfere with the pursuit of national interest. As John Courtney Murray says, the value of the traditional just war doctrine "is felt at the crucial point where the moral and political orders meet".[47] Since politics demands war and morality demands limits, and both politics and morality are necessary,

---

[46] Ramsey, _Just War_, p. 197.

[47] Murray, _MMW_, p. 17.

the two orders must be held together by creating the possibility of
limited war.[48] Sylvester Theisen too notes that unilateral rejection of
nuclear weapons is not militarily possible, and "morality like politics
deals with the possible".[49] Also, "In a pluralistic society, our national
policy in relation to nuclear weapons must be based on reason", so
Theisen does not adopt a religiously prophetic approach: "Attitudes that
are fiercely moralistic sound impressive in lectures and books but they
are dangerous in existential situations that require some kind of action."[50]

Paul Ramsey agrees. Twice in refuting Stein he adopts an argument
of Elizabeth Anscombe against pacifism to charge that nuclear pacifism
has produced great harm:

> Nuclear pacifism teaches people to make no
> distinction between the murderous and non-
> murderous intentions of men in support of
> deterrence. In this way nuclear pacifism has
> corrupted enormous numbers of people who will
> not act according to its tenets. They become
> convinced that in the matter of deterrence a
> number of things are wicked which are not;
> hence, seeing no way of avoiding 'wickedness,'
> they set no limits to it.[51]

Thus according to counterforce advocates, the nuclear pacifist
"witness" is dangerous whether accepted or rejected. Individuals may be
called to a noble pacifist vocation, but they must not demand it of the

---

[48]Ibid., p. 18.

[49]Sylvester Theisen, "Man and Nuclear Weapons," _The American Bene-dictine Review_, XIV (1963), 379. He does not explicate the word "possible".

[50]Ibid., p. 375.

[51]Ramsey, _Peace, Churches, Bomb_, p. 49; _Just War_, p. 364. Ramsey, like Anscombe, does not offer proof for this assertion or explain how people's actions are affected.

whole Church and certainly not of society.[52]

For their part, counterforce moralists would be content to contribute to a restoration of the just war tradition, which they admit has been little followed in this century not only by governments and nations but also by Christians.[53] They too would like the Church to speak with a united voice, but the message they urge is very different than that of the nuclear pacifists.

---

[52]James Dougherty, "The Christian and Nuclear Pacifism," Catholic World, CXCVIII (1964), 337-338.

[53]Murray, MMW, p. 15; Paul Ramsey, "Right and Wrong Calculation," The Moral Dilemma of Nuclear Weapons (New York, 1961), pp. 53-54; Ramsey, Just War, xi.

Chapter VI

CRITICISMS AND CONCLUSIONS

In the preceding chapters I have described the various aspects of
Christian nuclear pacifism as it is located in debate with alternate views.
At the same time I have given a reasonably complete picture of the counterforce position, which is also based on the just war tradition, and the bluff
position, which is not as fully articulated but which presumably bases its
rejection of the use or countervalue use of nuclear weapons on the just war
tradition. On this basis I will offer some observations and criticisms of
these three views. Then I will offer my conclusions about how the issue of
nuclear weapons has challenged the just war tradition as a whole.

Nuclear Pacifism: Criticisms and Agenda

Nuclear pacifists believe that their position is clearly required by
a serióus and honest application of the just war criteria to the question
of nuclear war. At the same time they claim that nuclear pacifism is com-
patible or even identical with simple common sense. However, after its
high point in the late 1950's and early 1960's nuclear pacifism waned among
both moralists and the general public, at least in terms of articulate
support. Only in the late 1970's and early 1980's has it again gained
more attention, but even now the classic earlier statements remain the
chief samples of nuclear pacifism. I suggest the following as some of the
reasons for its decline.

1) The whole issue of nuclear weapons itself received less attention
than previously. One reason is that after the Berlin and Cuban crises

passed without resulting in nuclear war, and Cold War tensions were eased somewhat, the high level of immediate fear of nuclear war also eased.[1] Secondly, with the end of atmospheric nuclear testing, concern for adverse domestic consequences from nuclear weapons also declined. However, in recent years the same two factors of fear and domestic consequences have served to refocus attention on nuclear weapons. The fear level has again been raised due to heightened East/West tensions, military build-ups on both sides, and increased talk of limited nuclear war which would be "won". In the United States, massive construction plans for the MX missile system and a rising defense budget in a time of domestic cutbacks have again high-lighted the domestic costs of nuclear weapons.

2) A second reason for the decline of nuclear pacifism is that it failed to offer a clear "solution" to the danger of nuclear war that was acceptable to a large proportion of the American people. In fact, since no clear and acceptable solution emerged to this complex issue, many people either ignored it or pinned whatever hopes they had on a policy of MAD and multilateral arms control. Only in England and other European countries which could not hope to match Soviet nuclear power did calls for unilateral disarmament gain much of a hearing.

3) In the 1960's those concerned with peace issues were most involved in the debate about the war in Vietnam. Social activists have also been preoccupied with other issues such as civil rights, human rights, poverty and world hunger, and various liberation movements.[2]

---

[1] In 1966 Walter Stein noted that "the world of the mid-sixties seems a lot less imminently explosive than that of a few years ago." Peace on Earth, p. 49.

[2] Cf. J. Bryan Hehir in Gessert and Hehir, NND, pp. 70-71.

4) Pacifism has enjoyed a resurgence and has attracted some people who might have been or remained nuclear pacifists. Even those who are not total pacifists may focus on arms control or preventing war rather than on defining what is morally permitted in war and deterrence.

5) Within the Roman Catholic Church there has been more emphasis on Scripture, and sometimes the discussion of war is carried on more in terms of Scripture than of the just war tradition.

These then are a few of the factors which contributed to the waning of nuclear pacifism. Current widespread concern with nuclear issues has given it new opportunity to regain prominence in moral thought and to put forward its view in the political arena. However, to date there has been a paucity of theologians and others to maintain and advance a nuclear pacifist position based on the just war criteria. As it is, the nuclear pacifism I have dealt with in this study exhibits certain weaknesses which must be addressed if it is to be strengthened as a moral position.

First of all, nuclear pacifists (in the specific sense) need to develop the basis on which they condemn all nuclear weapons. All just war theorists condemn the indiscriminate use of any weapon, and any kind of weapon may be used indiscriminately. Furthermore, as I noted in Chapter II, some nuclear pacifists do explicitly recognize that in particular instances nuclear weapons, even, in rare cases, large ones, might be used legitimately. Still, nuclear pacifists condemn all nuclear weapons because they assume that small nuclear weapons are the exception rather than the rule, that there are few occasions in which nuclear weapons could be justly used, and that it is unlikely that nuclear war could stay limited. They point to the huge stockpiles of nuclear weapons and judge it wrong to even risk all-out nuclear war.

While these are strong points, the condemnation of the use of any nuclear weapons, particularly the smallest ones, requires that the distinction between nuclear and conventional weapons be reinforced.[3] I would do so by making these points: In terms of the atomic processes they employ, all nuclear weapons are qualitatively distinct from other types of weapons, and the use of even the smallest ones can be detected with a geiger counter. The identification of nuclear weapons as a distinct class is already embedded in popular and technical language. At the same time there is a continuum of destructive power from the smallest to the largest nuclear weapons: there is no natural distinction between tactical, theatre, and strategic nuclear weapons. Thus any use of nuclear weapons crosses an objective, known, feared, and symbolically significant boundary with no natural limit, posing a serious risk of escalation. Even if there is no escalation, any use of nuclear weapons legitimates future use with its risk of escalation.[4]

In short, there are several links in the chain of argument by which nuclear pacifists may condemn all use of nuclear weapons: 1) The scientific/military/political/cultural (i.e. linguistic) identification of nuclear weapons as a category distinct from other categories of weapons. 2) The military/political judgment that any use of nuclear weapons runs a significant risk of the escalation of nuclear conflict, perhaps to the

---

[3]J. Bryan Hehir in Gessert and Hehir, NND, pp. 48-50, makes the same point. While he speaks of "psychological criteria" which distinguish nuclear and conventional weapons I also include scientific criteria he assumes.

[4]Ibid., p. 49. Of course, any limited use also sets a precedent for limited use, reducing the ominous symbolic meaning of crossing the conventional/nuclear "firebreak".

point of all-out nuclear war. 3) The moral judgment that most uses of nuclear weapons, and certainly the all-out use of them, would be immoral according to the just war criteria. 4) The moral judgment that even to risk extensive or all-out nuclear war is immoral. In this way the condemnation of a type of _weapons_ is ultimately hinged to the usual just war criteria governing a type of weapons _use_ (link three). A similar procedure might be used to condemn other types of weapons, such as chemical and biological.

Two things should be noted about this way of arguing. First, it might come into conflict with the just war criterion that only the minimum necessary force should be used. There might be cases in which a nuclear weapon could accomplish a military objective with less destruction than a conventional barrage. This type of reasoning should therefore not be employed carelessly in ruling out numerous types of weapons. Secondly, an honest casuistry should be open to changes in the first two links. For instance, if a scientific/military/political/cultural distinction arose to clearly separate a class of relatively tiny nuclear weapons from the others, they probably would have to be removed from condemnation as a class.

If nuclear pacifists need to strengthen their arguments for dealing with the lower end of the scale of nuclear violence, they also need to take a closer look at the middle range of that scale. As I have noted in the previous chapters, nuclear pacifists tend to base their arguments on the larger bombs and warheads, the targeting of cities, the use of large numbers of nuclear weapons, the policy of mutual assured destruction. Such an approach was understandable in the late 1950's and early 1960's when there was no sustained, public effort to implement in the West a counterforce strategic nuclear policy. But in recent years some strategic analysts and military and political leaders have given much more prominence to a counterforce policy. While it is true that Western governments have never repudiated the ultimate option of massive nuclear retaliation on an enemy society, a strictly counterforce nuclear policy for fighting and deterring war is a plausible alternative which nuclear pacifists should carefully address.

In popular writings the question is sometimes handled in this way: nuclear war is condemned as immoral and irrational because it would destroy civilization and perhaps the human race. When the idea of limited or counterforce warfare as an alternative to total war is raised, it is condemned for making nuclear war more likely. This is a switch to a different and perhaps contradictory argument. If nuclear war is immoral because it is vastly destructive, any attempt to limit it should be commended. If limited or counterforce options are wrong because they make nuclear war more likely, then perhaps the MAD policy should be advocated. Indeed, some recent authors have urged pacifists, nuclear pacifists, and those who accept the MAD system to join together to resist the theory of limited nuclear war.[5]

Of course, both the limitation and prevention of war are proper concerns. The question is how the two are related. Nuclear pacifists must allow the counterforce position to be judged first on its own merits according to the just war criteria before considering how it contributes to the

---

[5]E.g. John C. Bennett, "Countering the Theory of Limited Nuclear War," The Christian Century, January 7-14, 1981, p. 10. I assume that by "mutual nuclear deterrence" he means the MAD policy. Bennett's arguments seem to logically imply the bluff position but he does not make this explicit.

likelihood of war. Such an account should reckon with changing military situations. For instance, one factor that would favor a counterforce argument today is that nuclear missiles, particularly those based on land, are much more accurate than they were in the 1960's. On the other hand, because many targets have been "hardened" (placed underground and protected with steel and concrete), weapons of greater destructive power are necessary to destroy them. Also, both the Western and Soviet blocs continue to build up their nuclear arsenals and thus to increase the number of counterforce targets.

It is not my purpose here to enter into the actual evaluation of counterforce nuclear warfare. I would simply offer the judgment that nuclear pacifists need not rely on massive countercity warfare to prove their case. The most obvious fact is that nuclear weapons produce radiation which is inherently indiscriminate, posing a threat not only to noncombatants in the opposing society but also to citizens of neutral countries. Theodore Weber admits that if the nuclear deterrent is ever used, "Even if the missiles are controlled exactly to the targets, the radioactive fallout will be carried around the world."[6]

While nuclear pacifists have occasionally analyzed the over-all effects of counterforce warfare, what is seldom done is to examine specific examples of possible counterforce uses of nuclear weapons. Francis Winters briefly does so (Ford and Winters, ENS?, p. 150) when he cites a U.S. study which estimates that if the Soviets used two three-megaton warheads on each of the 150 silos at Whiteman Air Force Base in Missouri, 10.3 million civilians would be killed. Other examples of a lesser use of force

---

[6]Theodore Weber, Modern War and the Pursuit of Peace, p. 20.

should also be studied. Such information might be difficult to obtain, and
even if it were there would not be a military/political context to allow a
full analysis. Nevertheless any steps that were taken along this line
would help to concretize a vague counterforce idea so that it could be sub-
jected to closer scrutiny. At the same time, of course, nuclear pacifism
would be more open to criticism, but also more compelling since it would
have to rely less on assuming the worst case. Such a procedure might also
allow, if not require, more interaction between moralists, strategic
analysts, political scientists, physicians, and others.

I have stated that nuclear pacifists need to strengthen their arguments for condemning all nuclear weapons and that they need to look more
closely at counterforce nuclear warfare. My third comment is that nuclear
pacifism will erode its own foundation unless it can broaden and deepen
its position. Nuclear pacifism of the type I am concerned with is based
on the just war tradition, which affirms the legitimacy of some wars and
types of military actions and (presumably) denies others. Because nuclear
pacifists dwell on the negation of modern war, their affirmation may easily
be overlooked. Thus they may contribute to the claim of some opponents of
modern war that the just war theory is "irrelevant" to the present era.
Those who make that claim really mean that it is unable to justify modern
war; the distinction is important because nuclear pacifists base their
negation precisely on the just war tradition. Similarly, nuclear pacifists
may contribute to the idea that our present need is to "abolish war".
While the just war tradition and the goal of abolishing war are not necessarily incompatible, there is certainly a difference in mood. Nuclear
pacifists may be reluctant to spell out when war may be justified if the
goal is to abolish war. Nevertheless, nuclear pacifists cannot specify

when war is not justified unless they say when it is justified. Nuclear pacifists who depend upon the just war tradition cannot assume that it will always be there as a starting point unless they do more to maintain its vitality.

One way in which this may be done is to apply the just war criteria to various types of conventional warfare, including not only international conflict but also revolution, counterinsurgency warfare, the actions of an international or world police force, and so forth. Most nuclear pacifists have done little work in these areas. Such analysis is necessary not only for the sake of the just war tradition itself but also because most nuclear pacifists have said little about what policies they would advocate in regard to conventional armaments. Even those nuclear pacifists who believe that major conventional warfare is too risky as long as one or both sides possess nuclear weapons would not rule out all use of force, so they could still show the relevance of the just war criteria. Michael Walzer in his book Just and Unjust Wars: A Moral Argument with Historical Illustrations (New York, 1977) provides a good model for an attempt to formulate a comprehensive just war theory.

Sometimes in contemporary ethics there seem to be two separate streams in the discussion about war. On the one hand there is the debate between pacifists and just war theorists along traditional lines with little if any recognition of the problems of modern warfare. On the other hand there is the discussion about nuclear weapons. Nuclear pacifists could help to unite these two streams if they broadened their approach as I have suggested. At the same time they would have to deepen their argument by exploring the roots of the just war tradition in natural law, Western and church history, and Scripture, for nuclear pacifists face a serious challenge from pacifism, which claims as its basis the Christian New Testament. Of course nuclear pacifists offer what they would consider clear advantages over pacifism, such as a justification for self-defense and the use of violence by domestic police. Only by entering more fully into the debate with pacifism as well as with other views will nuclear pacifism be able to defend its own foundations.[7]

My fourth general comment raises the question of how firmly nuclear pacifists are willing to hold to their position as an unconditional commitment even in the face of possible or probable dire consequences. In the fifteen or twenty years since the height of nuclear pacifism the nuclear threshhold has never been crossed, contrary to the predictions or fears of nuclear pacifists. Perhaps this indicates that the nuclear deterrent has "worked", just as mutual deterrence probably worked to prevent the use of poison gas during World War II. On the other hand, it is still possible that unilateral nuclear disarmament, at least by the United States, could lead to nuclear blackmail by other countries and perhaps even war, nuclear or conventional.

Nuclear pacifists have addressed some of these questions partly by countering that reliance on nuclear weapons poses greater dangers than commitment to unilateral disarmament. What they have not sufficiently faced, however, is the possibility or probability that nuclear pacifism may yield unhappy consequences while at the same time it fails to become public policy and thus to reduce the existing dangers of the nuclear

---

[7] One nuclear pacifist who does strongly criticize pacifism is Elizabeth Anscombe in "War and Murder," pp. 51-57.

arsenal. For instance, a strong movement for unilaterialism in the NATO countries could reduce the incentive of the Soviet Union for multilateral arms control.[8] Also, if unilateralism gained a lot of support in the United States (and perhaps elsewhere), it could lead to a militaristic counterreaction, domestic turmoil, political repression, even armed revolt. Even without a mass movement, some individuals who hold nuclear pacifist convictions may face hardships of various kinds because of their refusal to aid in the production of nuclear weapons, enter the armed services, pay war taxes, and so forth. In times of tension and of course in time of war social and official sanctions would increase.

Of course, I am here looking only at the dark side of the picture. It may be that nuclear pacifism has contributed something toward reducing Cold War tensions, preventing the use of nuclear weapons, and reaching agreements which control the testing, proliferation, and stockpiling of nuclear weapons. Furthermore, it is always possible that in the future the world will be spared a nuclear holocaust if even one person at a crucial moment decides not to turn the key or push the button that would fire a nuclear missile. Nuclear pacifists are fully entitled to point out the dangers of current nuclear policies and the benefits of their own position, and to join in political coalitions which advocate, for instance, multilateral disarmament. But it is a requirement of simple honesty that those who lead in advocating nuclear pacifism continue, as they have in the past, to admit that commitment to it might entail suffering with no

---

[8]This is suggested by Walter Laqueur, "Hollanditis: A New Stage in European Neutralism," Commentary, August, 1981, p. 26. To date it seems, however, that European nuclear protest has put strong pressure on both the United States and the Soviet Union to at least appear anxious to reduce nuclear weapons in Europe.

visible results. This will probably reduce nuclear pacifism's political viability, but it will reduce the number of those who abandon or turn against it when it becomes costly.

It is difficult for individuals to sustain this kind of commitment, and the hope on which it is based, without a supportive community. Not only courage but patience is needed. There are innumerable formal and informal expressions of "community", and many of them may be helpful. All Christian nuclear pacifists, however, must be concerned about the Christian Church in all its forms. They especially need to clarify what they hope and expect of church authorities at the denominational level (including here the Roman Catholic Church). Do nuclear pacifists wish to encourage official pluralism, the support of nuclear pacifism with tolerance for other views, or the official endorsement of nuclear pacifism? Many nuclear pacifists would probably opt for official support of their position with tolerance for other views. This could cause a great deal of controversy if taken seriously in a denomination. But before it could be taken seriously by local church members, nuclear pacifists would have to help educate their churches about the issue. In many denominations such an effort would have to overcome the fact that there has been little attempt to teach members the basic principles of the just war tradition, much less how it relates to nuclear and other modern weapons. Nuclear pacifists should spend at least as much effort trying to convince their own church members to adopt this position as they do trying to convince government leaders and citizens at large. If significant portions of the churches are not willing to accept it, why should society pay any attention to Christian nuclear pacifism?

Paul Ramsey's Justification of Nuclear War and Deterrence

My comments on nuclear pacifism suggest an agenda for further work rather than a fundamental criticism of the position itself. In my judgment the counterforce position is much more seriously flawed. Rather than discuss it in general terms I will critique the argument of Paul Ramsey, who provides the most full and careful exposition of the counterforce view. I will discuss first his theory about the use of nuclear weapons in fighting a war and type B deterrence which depends upon it. Then I will offer some criticisms about his general approach.

One of the main themes of Paul Ramsey's work on nuclear war is that we must begin with what it is morally and rationally possible to do in fighting a war. Thus the will and ability to fight a counterforce nuclear war is at the same time "type A" nuclear deterrence, and all deterrence except that based on the bluff (type D) is built upon it.

As I noted in Chapter III, in his 1961 book War and the Christian Conscience Ramsey had doubts about the morality and utility of any but the smallest nuclear weapons. While he felt that as a moralist he could not determine the needs of counterforce warfare, he placed the burden of proof clearly on those who would justify the utility of megaton and at least the upper ranges of kiloton weapons (pp. 291-292), and he saw no need for a stockpile of megaton weapons (pp. 299-301). He favored Thomas Murray's plan of what Ramsey called "unilateral megatonnage disarmament" (p. 299, author's italics). Thus in his early formulation Ramsey suggested that a counterforce policy could set significant limits on not only the targeting but the size and numbers of nuclear weapons. Later, however, when he allowed the possibility of the deterrence of bluff, all limits based on counterforce targeting were removed, with the only remaining limit being the utility of the threat for the bluff itself.

Even apart from the bluff, however, Ramsey later seemed to allow much more leeway in the size and perhaps the number of nuclear weapons. He defends the possible discriminating use of "counter-force nuclear strikes in an age when there are military establishments fifty or more miles in diameter and legitimate targets deeply buried".[9] Ramsey does not say what size nuclear weapon he has in mind for these targets, but in his later writings he only flatly rules out the 100 megaton bomb.[10] Neither does Dr. Ramsey ever state what information he has about how many missiles of what sizes each side has, how many military targets there might be in the Soviet Union, and so forth. I doubt that there have ever been many fifty-mile military establishments. On the other hand, there are certainly thousands of missile sites in the Soviet Union today, and many of them are "hardened" and so require powerful nuclear weapons for their destruction. If these are considered legitimate targets, and if ample allowance is granted for the possibility that a large percentage of the strategic arsenal might be wiped out by an opponent's first strike, there seems to be little practical moral limit on the number of nuclear weapons allowed by the counterforce doctrine. Below I will question the justification of counterforce warfare. Here I simply want to note that Ramsey's view after 1961 places few if any limits on the size and number of nuclear weapons.

---

[9] Ramsey, Just War, p. 408.

[10] Ramsey, Just War, p. 329. Because 100 megatons is the example used by Lawler (Peace, Churches, Bomb, p. 34), it is not necessarily true that Ramsey would justify the possession of weapons up to 100 megatons.

Even in terms of his later and seemingly more relaxed judgments about the legitimate counterforce possibilities of the nuclear arsenal, Ramsey seems rather casual in his assessment of actual Western targeting. In response to Walter Stein's question about how many present forces are directed to restricted military targets, Ramsey replies: "I venture that the correct answer is: most of the forces have counter-force targets on such alternate use."[11] Apparently Ramsey admits that some nuclear forces are targeted on cities exclusively and others have dual targeting including cities. Any careful application of the principle of discrimination, which Ramsey considers to be so basic, should require severe criticism of such a policy. But Ramsey merely concludes: "We need to clean up our deterrence system, of course; but mainly we need to clean up our notions of deterrence and of what we erroneously suppose this depends upon."[12]

The central notion which Ramsey wishes to clean up is that deterrence necessarily depends upon the intention to commit murder by attacking cities. Other than the ability to destroy an opponent's military targets, the first type of legitimate deterrence (type B) which Ramsey identifies is that based on collateral civilian damage. This is a peculiar use of language. A building may be damaged, and one might say that a person who is injured has suffered "damage." But a person who is killed is definitely not "damaged." It is one of the euphemisms of the nuclear age to describe the death of thousands or even millions of people as "collateral civilian

---

[11] Ramsey, Peace, Churches, Bomb, p. 48. Quoting Stein, Peace, Churches, Bomb, p. 24. Stein was referring to Bishop Hannan's argument at Vatican II that there exist nuclear weapons with "a very precise limit of destruction" such as one with a range of 1.3 to 2.5 miles and a force of 40 tons of TNT. For Ramsey to extend the argument to all counterforce targeting, especially in the context of deterrence, is very misleading.

[12] Ramsey, Peace, Churches, Bomb, p. 47. Ramsey is here defending the morality of deterrence against Stein; in other contexts he is more critical of strictly countervalue deterrence.

damage." However, I will employ the term here because Ramsey uses it in a technical sense to mean the indirect and unintended harm which is inflicted on civilians in the course of attacking a military target.

Type B deterrence depends, of course, upon the moral justification of civilian harm inflicted during the course of counterforce warfare. Before I can question that justification it is necessary to clear away a methodological issue raised by Ramsey. That will require some close analysis, particularly of a dialogue between Justus George Lawler and Paul Ramsey in Peace, the Churches and the Bomb and Ramsey's follow-up article, "Again, the Justice of Deterrence" in The Just War, pp. 314-366.

In furtherance of his suggestion that it is immoral to stockpile more nuclear weapons than have legitimate military targets, Lawler calculated that in a full-scale counterforce war 15,000 megatons of force would be unleashed against Russia and that nearly all of the Russian people would be killed. He concluded: "Obviously we have gone beyond any calculation of double effect. Nothing within the scope of man's imagination would render just such devastation and murder." (Peace, Churches, Bomb, p. 35) Ramsey corrected his account by saying that such a war would be wrong because disproportionate; it would not be "murder" because it would not violate the principle of non-combatant immunity (Peace, Churches, Bomb, p. 54). Lawler replied that the principle of proportion is "implicit" in the principle of double effect and that if I kill a thousand innocent civilians in the act of killing one combatant it is murder, for I obviously do not intend to kill only the combatant (Peace, Churches, Bomb, p. 88). Ramsey in turn agreed that this would be murder, but because the intention was directed to non-combatants in the first place, not because of any principle of proportion in double effect. He noted, however, that such action would be justified if the lone combatant were a commander about to effect the destruction of a city of a hundred thousand people. (Just War, pp. 350,355) According to Ramsey only the direct, intended killing of non-combatants is murder. If non-combatants are unavoidably killed during an attack on a (reasonably important) military target, this is justified by the principle of double effect, which contains no principle of proportion. If such killing is disproportionate to the military/political good achieved, it is equally sinful but not (on that account) murder (cf. Just War, pp. 347-349).

We can unpack this dispute by noting three points: First of all, there are various ways in which the word "proportionality" may be used. Three uses are germane here. As I noted in Chapter II, the fourth criterion of the principle of double effect is that the good effects of an action must be proportionate to the evil effects. Ramsey himself explicitly says this in War and the Christian Conscience, p. 48. Apparently it is Ramsey's desire to avoid calling disproportionate damage "murder" that has led him later to say (erroneously) that there is no criterion of proportion in the principle of double effect. The only sense in which Ramsey here thinks of the principle of proportion is the criterion for evaluating the good and evil effects of a war as a whole. Lawler is thinking of proportionality in still a third sense as an objective determinate of subjective intention. Thus Ramsey has a point when he says that Lawler's example of killing one thousand non-combatants to get at one combatant can be discussed in terms of the agent's intention. Both Lawler and Ramsey agree that such an act would be murder (assuming the one were an ordinary soldier), but they disagree on whether the determining factor may be called a "principle of proportion." I think that because a comparison of numbers is involved here it is logical for Lawler to use the word "proportion", but in view of other uses of the term it may be too confusing.

It seems that Ramsey and Lawler disagree not only on the use of this term but also on whether the destruction of nearly all of the people of Russia in a counterforce attack would be analogous to killing one thousand civilians to kill one ordinary soldier. If they agreed they would both call it murder. Though "murder" or "mass murder" may properly describe an act of, for instance, a direct nuclear strike against a city, perhaps it is stretching the term "murder" to apply it to an entire war, consisting of numerous individual military actions. It would be better to use the phrase "murderous war".

A similar question is whether it is appropriate to consider counterforce war as a single action to be judged by the principle of double effect as a whole. Lawler does so, and as I noted in Chapter II, some nuclear pacifists and counterforce theorists do so as well. Even Ramsey does so in War and the Christian Conscience (pp. 256-257). When used in this way, it is a useful shorthand way of indicating a war characterized by counterforce actions which may be justified by the principle of double effect. But such use of the categories may contribute to confusion, as in the case of the Lawler-Ramsey debate, because when a war is considered as a single action, the principle (or principles, if Lawler's usage be adopted) of proportion within the principle of double effect become co-extensive with the just war criterion that the good effects of a war must outweigh its evil effects. In technical moral casuistry such merging of the categories should be avoided for the sake of clarity.

My own conclusions about the Lawler-Ramsey debate on the use of the term "murder" may be summarized as follows: 1) A principle of proportion-

ality is implicit in the second term of the principle of double effect as
an objective measure of subjective intention, though probably the word
"proportionality" should not be used. Any action in which the killing of
civilians vastly outweighs military objectives should be considered murder.
2) When the two effects are roughly comparable, a principle of proportionality comes into play as the fourth criterion of the principle of double
effect. Even when judged disproportionate, a military action cannot be
called "murder" if weighty reasons can be given for it. Thus rather than
a dichotomy between murder and the unintended, indirect killing of the innocent, I would identify between them the third category of actions which
are not justified by the principle of double effect because their effects
are disproportionate. 3) This still leaves a large gray area between
actions that are clearly murder and those which are disproportionate
according to the principle of double effect. 4) This third category is
a large part of the just means criterion that the military importance of a
particular target must be proportionate to the evil done in attacking it.
However, an action might be entirely counterforce and yet disproportionate
by this criterion. For instance, it might not be worthwhile to lose
fifty thousand soldiers to capture a small enemy stronghold. When a distinction in types of disproportionate action is important it is generally
clear in the context. Therefore for practical purposes the third category
above may simply be described as a disproportionate act.

Much more is involved here than technical moral semantics. The whole
issue of determining what is and what is not murder is important for Ramsey
because he believes that a prospective act or murder can be much more easily
identified than a prospective disproportionate act, since the determination
of whether an act can be justified by the principle of proportion can be

made only in a specific situation in which the conditions and consequences of the action may be weighed.[13] Thus the more narrowly murder can be defined, the more room there is for the accumulation of nuclear weapons. Ramsey believes that many or most of the upper ranges of destruction that would result from counterforce nuclear warfare would be disproportionate,[14] but because a present immoral intention cannot be proven, the deployment of a vast nuclear arsenal cannot be condemned. This allows Ramsey to claim that there may be an effective nuclear deterrent within the bounds of counterforce targeting. Thus in Ramsey's theory while the principle of proportion might serve soon to condemn actual nuclear war, it acts late in condemning the present nuclear deterrent.

Still, since even extensive counterforce warfare is so likely to be disproportionate, Ramsey must justify threatening nuclear war for the sake of deterrence, and he does so in two ways. The first, which corresponds closely to what I said in the previous paragraph about the situational aspect of proportionality, is that governments have the responsibility to prepare for any eventuality and must be given an ample margin of error in doing so.[15] The second justification is via the bluff of the "disproportionate threat". Since this has a different logic than the first, it is surprising how quickly Ramsey employs it.[16] Perhaps this shows how con-

---

[13] Ramsey, Peace, Churches, Bomb, p. 55.

[14] Ibid., pp. 46, 54.

[15] Ramsey, Peace, Churches, Bomb, pp. 53, 54. The first part of the statement is more implicit than explicit.

[16] E.g. Ramsey, Just War, p. 347.

scious he is that nuclear warfare may quickly become disproportionate.

Later I will offer some comments about taking risks, allowing a great deal of discretion to the government, and the deterrence of bluff which will undermine Ramsey's two justifications for making threats which are (or are likely to be) disproportionate. My point here will be that acceptance of the counterforce position would require a much closer application of both of the just war criteria of discrimination and proportionality than Ramsey provides.

The validity of the whole counterforce theory depends upon the ability to justify the use of nuclear weapons on particular targets. Yet for all his military/political sophistication Ramsey makes very little effort to take sample cases of particular targets and examine whether the use of particular sizes of nuclear weapons to destroy them would be licit. No doubt this in part reflects a lack of readily available information of this kind in the strategic literature, but Ramsey makes little use of even the kind of examples that are available. Some of the cases he does mention are open to serious question. For example, the destruction of vast military installations which are fifty miles in diameter, as mentioned above, could probably not be accomplished without such great amounts of fallout that it would be disproportionate.[17]

Also, Ramsey claims that it does not violate the principle of discrimination to destroy missile bases and command posts located in or near cities.[18] In fact, he goes so far as to say that because of such military installations Omaha and other American cities "are now legitimate military

---

[17] Ramsey himself seems to recognize this in discussing Lawler's example of counterforce warfare. Ramsey, Peace, Churches, Bomb, p. 15.

[18] Ramsey, Just War, pp. 213, 437-438, 481, 509. In all but the first case the topic under discussion is counter-insurgency warfare.

targets."[19]   Ramsey's point here is that the enemy cannot use the principle of noncombatant immunity to his own military advantage; when he tries
to do so, it is the enemy who is at fault for enlarging the target, not
the one who must cause extensive collateral damage to destroy the target.
But here the domestic analogy used by Ramsey and other just war theorists
is relevant.   Just as it is immoral to deter or punish criminals by threatening or attacking their family members, so it is immoral (though a low
degree of murder) to kill a criminal by shooting through the family members
he has wrongfully used as a shield.   Similarly it is murder to destroy a
city in the process of attacking a military installation.   To deny this
Ramsey must either abandon the deontological status of noncombatant immunity
or give it an extremely loose interpretation.   That he gives it a very
loose interpretation is indicated by his statement that "in tactical bombing, the destruction of a considerable part of the area might be incidental
to the destruction of the target," even if such "incidental" destruction
killed millions of civilians.[20]   Because the lives of noncombatants must
be so heavily weighted, and so many would be killed (not to mention other
harm), and because so little could be accomplished by it, I would consider
such military action to be so disproportionate that it would be murderous.

Even if the military examples are only considered disproportionate
rather than murderous, they still do not meet the just war criteria, so
such forms of counterforce warfare would not be moral according to the

---

[19]Ibid., p. 213.

[20]Ramsey, War and the Christian Conscience, p. 65. Many Europeans
today are not quite so willing to justify the "incidental" destruction of
their homelands in tactical nuclear war. For information about the effects
of counterforce and other types of nuclear war on the United States and
the Soviet Union, see Office of Technology Assessment of the Congress of
the United States, The Effects of Nuclear War (Washington, D.C., 1979).

just war tradition. Of course, there are other examples of smaller and/or
more isolated targets that would better fit Ramsey's case, but these would
have to be offered for close scrutiny before they could be properly judged.

Just as in the case of individual targets and tactical warfare, so
Ramsey and other counterforce theorists need to attempt a closer reckoning
of when strategic nuclear war as a whole might be considered proportionate.
As I noted earlier in the chapter, Ramsey agrees with Lawler that no con-
ceivable reason would justify killing nearly all of the people of Russia.
Francis Winters, on the other hand, says that the loss of six million
Americans would be disproportionate to any conceivable political goal.[21]
As gross as these figures are (in more than one sense), at least there is
a basis for discussion of what might be justly proportionate damage.

The counterforce theory of nuclear warfare itself raises a new
question for the principle of proportionality. Let us consider the case
of a contemplated second-strike attack on the nuclear forces of the Soviet
Union, which has already fired two-thirds of its ICBM's. Since (let us
assume) it is not known which Soviet missiles have been fired, most of
their silos will be empty (at least in those cases where there is only
one missile per silo). If those cases are taken individually, hardly any
collateral damage is justified since the targets now have little military
value. Even if the total attack is considered, there is decreased military utility of the remaining Soviet strategic force, yet collateral damage
would remain the same as if the silos were all full. Could such damage
be justified? Counterforce theorists should deal with this new challenge

---

[21] Ford and Winters, ENS?, p. 151. Since different countries are in
view, the question arises whether the lives of "enemy" populations are to
be valued as highly as those of our own citizens.

it poses for the principle of proportionality.

These criticisms of the justification of actual counterforce warfare also pose problems for types A and B deterrence which depend upon it. Even if counterforce nuclear warfare could be fully justified, however, there would remain a serious problem with Ramsey's account of type B deterrence. In his view one wants the deterring effects of an unwanted side-effect (collateral civilian damage) of counterforce warfare. Stein and Ramsey are right to debate the types and moral culpability of "wanting" (cf. Chapter III), but the most basic gauge of intention is (as Ramsey shows) how one acts. And here Ramsey's view pulls deterrence policy in two opposite directions. The whole thrust of the just war tradition is to reduce the harm that is done, particularly to noncombatants even at heavy cost to military personnel. On the other hand, Ramsey is very concerned for the needs of deterrence, which requires a threat of maximum collateral civilian damage. It is clear that Ramsey chooses to maximize the threat, for he speaks of "counterforces warfare in its maximum form"[22] and he would justify the deterrence of bluff (type D) only if types B and C cannot be _made_ effective.[23] The only limit is that any unnecessary extension of the target or increase in collateral damage would violate the principle of discrimination and thus be a sign of a murderous intention.

---

[22] Ramsey, Just War, p. 252. In Just War, p. 347, Ramsey relates this to what I have considered the bluff of a threat of something disproportionate. The fact that Ramsey ties maximum counterforce to a form of bluff may indicate his awareness that the needs of type B deterrence pull in the opposite direction of the just war tradition, which would seek to minimize collateral civilian damage.

[23] Ibid., p. 254, author's italics.

Since Ramsey allows such a loose application of the principle of discrimination, there could be a lot of difference in targeting, size and type of weapons, number of weapons, and so forth depending upon whether one chose to maximize or minimize collateral civilian damage. The fact that nuclear policy may be pulled in two different directions shows that only a long cord, stretched to the maximum, ties type B deterrence to the actual requirements of counterforce nuclear war as governed by just war criteria. In fact we may wonder if the upward pull of deterrence needs has not itself contributed to Ramsey's permissive attitude toward what may be done in counterforce warfare.

Regarding Ramsey's type C deterrence, which is based on the enemy's uncertainty that we will not use nuclear weapons on cities, I will make only two brief points. The first is that because Ramsey associates it with a government-declared policy that nuclear weapons will not be used against cities, it flatly contradicts any policy of countercity bluff. Secondly, Ramsey undermines his own argument. His whole point in discussing deterrent effects types B and C is to show that a counterforce deterrent may be effective. He says that type C is effective because the enemy cannot know that we will not go to countercity attacks, even though it is irrational. At the same time, he urges the West to trust the rationality of the opponent and not be deterred by the risk of counter-value war. The tension illustrates the strategic paradox in the era of mutual deterrence: If nuclear deterrence works, it works to deter our side, and so the opponent will not be deterred.

Paul Ramsey's Approach to the Nuclear Issue

Below I will discuss the bluff position, including Ramsey's statement
of it. At this point I will offer some broader criticisms of Ramsey's
approach. First, there is Ramsey's contention that moralists and church
bodies can speak only in terms of moral principles rather than drawing
conclusions based on assessment of fact. If this were true, no moralists
or church bodies could, in that capacity, advocate nuclear pacifism on
the basis of the just war tradition. Neither could they advocate the
counterforce position. Ramsey himself makes all kinds of factual judgments in the course of advocating the counterforce view. While he admits
that "any moral argument must have facts interwoven with the moral reasoning",[24] the facts must be stated hypothetically and the argument must not
rely on them. It is difficult to see how facts can be interwoven in an
argument and yet carry no weight.

I would make four points about this question. First, there is no
such thing as a moral issue that can be separated out from all facts.
One cannot even begin to talk about an issue without some assumptions of
fact. Secondly, moralists may get their "facts" from the general culture,
the mass media, or experts of various kinds, but whatever facts they use
should be open to challenge. Thirdly, some factual questions may be too
detailed or too specialized for moralists to judge. Only at that point
do they need to state facts in hypothetical form or withdraw the argument
to a more general level. Just when that point is reached will have to be
determined in the individual situation. In the case of nuclear weapons I

---

[24] Ramsey, Just War, p. 337.

judge that on the basis of the just war tradition the moralist can make several judgments before that level is reached. Fourthly, moralists and church bodies may at times need to distinguish what they believe to be certain moral judgments from less certain ones. This will depend partially on the nature of the facts involved in the argument.

For Ramsey, the issue is not so much one of competence as of office: the moralist or church body per se can only comment in moral terms on the moral issue in public questions,[25] while the citizen or statesman must carry through to particular judgments. To this I would reply that while not all the issues in a public question are moral issues, the moral issue of nuclear war is a public question. A moralist can judge that certain things are not moral issues, and so he or she has no particular competence to speak to them. But nuclear war is a public moral issue. Therefore a moralist cannot as Ramsey says distinguish him or herself as a moralist from him or herself as a citizen. Similarly, one cannot divide him or herself as (in this case) Christian and as citizen or statesman.

In summary, according to Ramsey a moralist (or church body) cannot rest a moral judgment on facts or make political judgments. In my view, moral argument must use facts and the moral and political aspects of nuclear war cannot be separated. Thomas Merton has called nuclear war "the most crucial moral and religious problem in twenty centuries of history",[26] and it would be strange indeed if moralists could not render judgment about it.

---

[25]Ibid.

[26]Thomas Merton, "Christian Ethics and Nuclear War," The Nonviolent Alternative, ed. Gordon Zahn (New York: Farrar, Straus, Giroux), p. 82.

Dr. Ramsey in theory limits the role of moralists to speaking of moral principles, but he also gives that role a particular orientation. He believes that the job of the moralist is to allow statesmen as much room as possible to employ force in the exercise of their responsibilities. As far as Christianity is concerned, he believes that the just war tradition itself is based on charity, and at crucial points he interprets it in such a way that Christian statesmen may have wide latitude to exercise their Christian charity through the employment of force for political purposes. However, those of us who are less impressed with the potential of nuclear weapons to be instruments of Christian charity might ask whether this is the proper orientation. Many Christian just war proponents today acknowledge that because of the prima facie obligation not to kill, the just war tradition was adopted to specify when an exception to that rule might be allowed. Therefore the burden of proof should be on those who would justify any form of killing, rather than on those who would withhold any option from the statesman.

Part of the reason Ramsey allows so much presumption to government leaders is that he wants the just war theory to be relevant to political and military decisions and effective in actually shaping those decisions. In order to meet these goals it must be a general ethic, not limited only to Christians. These goals of relevance, effectiveness, and generality require comment.

The irony of relevance is that if to be relevant means to be useful and acceptable, the just war tradition risks becoming irrelevant no matter how Ramsey applies it. If it is so acceptable that it makes no demands upon people, it might be "useful" as a justification of present policy, but even that becomes doubtful. For Ramsey just war morality and political prudence correspond so closely that one wonders why moral language is necessary at all: Political scientists and strategic analysts might better stick with the language of political and strategic needs without any recourse to the criteria of the just war tradition. On the other hand, whenever Ramsey does interpret the just war tradition as making substantive military/political demands, the demands may be criticized as being unacceptable and thus not useful in decision-making. For instance, Ramsey and John Courtney Murray have stated that a nation must be prepared to surrender rather than engage in all-out nuclear war. Murray indicated how acceptable that was when he complained that the United States Senate had voted eighty-two to two to deny government funds to any person or institution who ever proposed or conducted a study regarding the surrender of the United States government.[27] And Ramsey himself once noted that "Only a 'tragic gambler' will find it credible to believe an apparently surrendering enemy is not trying to gain time to inflict still greater damage."[28]

Ramsey and other counterforce advocates thus risk either making such low demands of the nuclear powers that the just war tradition becomes irrelevant to guiding policy or of making such (relatively) high demands that it can only be a minority position. Their attempts to find a middle ground fail not only because of the current political climate but because the logic of force combined with nuclear technology allows so little room for a middle ground. The best chance which counterforce advocates have of finding a middle ground, though, is precisely their central point that

---

[27] Murray, Morality and Modern War, p. 16.

[28] Paul Ramsey, "Dream and Reality in Deterrence and Defense," Christianity and Crisis, XXI (1961), 230.

civilians must never be attacked directly. While criticized by some military/political analysts and leaders, this demand gains sympathy from others. If applied, it might save millions of lives in a nuclear war. However, Ramsey at least has used the criterion so loosely that in many cases it would make little or no difference.

In their efforts to find a relevant and effective middle ground for the morality of warfare, Ramsey and other counterforce advocates reject the minority ethical status of the "sect". However, they acknowledge that the just war tradition has been neglected and often ignored in church and society in modern times. They thus champion a minority ethic which has the majority perspective of controlling society. While counterforce advocates do seek to (re)establish their interpretation of the just war tradition as the prevailing view, it seems that what they oppose is not minority status per se but the kind of minority status that would cause a rupture with the larger political society by rejecting the use of force as in pacifism or of significant kinds of force as in nuclear pacifism. This orientation itself casts doubt on whether counterforce advocates would ever be prepared to interpret the just war tradition in a way that required a break with the prevailing military/political posture. Any of their views which have the potential for causing such a break, as in regard to surrender or the necessity of military personnel to refuse to assist in murderous wartime actions, relate to the future and therefore remain untested. A counterforce position taken seriously, however, would demand some acts of resistance even before a war as long as countervalue actions remained an option. For instance, military personnel should refuse to even consider the optional targeting of cities. However, counterforce advocates have never counselled such acts of refusal.

Criticisms of the Bluff Position

The third position which I have described in the preceding chapters is deterrence based on the bluff. What is threatened but not intended may be countervalue nuclear warfare, as expressed by Paul Ramsey, or any use of nuclear weapons whatsoever, as advocated by J. Bryan Hehir and the American bishops. Ramsey's idea of the threat of something that would be disproportionate to do may also be considered a form of bluff, though he does not use that term for it.

Before discussing the bluff position itself, I would note that when Ramsey attempts to justify this type of deterrence it is part of a process of shifting the grounds for his argument about the morality of nuclear deterrence. At the beginning of the symposium Peace, the Churches, and the Bomb, Walter Stein attempted to prove that the statement and intentions of military and political leaders indicated a present actual countervalue deterrence policy. Ramsey disregarded that by saying that the real issue was the objective needs of deterrence, which could be met by a counterforce policy. When, on the other hand, Ramsey considered that the objective needs of deterrence might include a countervalue threat, he justified it by saying that in actual subjective intention military and political leaders might be bluffing. He supported the idea that actual intentions were limited to counterforce options by what he learned at a cocktail party in Washington, D.C. (Just War, p. 342). Of course, not all citizens can attend Washington cocktail parties so they must base their judgments on the statements of leaders. Since these statements included immoral threats, Ramsey pointed to the moral subjective intentions of the citizens. In short, whenever his position was challenged Ramsey shifted the ground of his argument to support the morality of nuclear deterrence. The necessity of these shifts casts doubt on the validity of his arguments at each stage.

The first direct comment I have about the bluff position is that there is no way to measure its influence in government or in military or strategic circles. While a few people may be willing to openly advocate this position, I assume that most or all of the people in high authority who held such a view would be unwilling to say so openly. By its very nature a bluff position cannot be policy or the threat would lose much of its validity. This fact in turn raises serious questions about the possibilities of employing such a position in a democracy.

It is hypothetically conceivable for top military and political leaders to secretly plan never to order indiscriminate or disproportionate nuclear warfare, or in fact any kind of nuclear warfare. Perhaps individual lower-level military personnel can hold a similar resolution, assuming they have enough information to know what military activities they are helping to carry out. But citizens cannot have such an intention because their fingers are not on the "button". Their only role is to help shape military/political policy. For citizens to simply trust their leaders to do right when the time comes even though they make wrong threats in the present is to abandon the responsibility they are assumed to have in a democracy to help shape policy on critical issues. According to Ramsey, for a viable deterrence of bluff, citizens need only politically sustain a government's "possible willingness" to commit genocide.[29] Even this minimal statement of the requirements of an effective deterrent involves a willingness

---

[29]Ramsey, Just War, p. 363, author's italics. Of course, Ramsey held this position only temporarily. He states why he rejected it in a letter to the editor of Newsweek, July 5, 1982.

to leave open the option of genocide, and thus there is a conditional
murderous intention on the part of citizens who do not ojbect to such a
government policy. If I am right, the bluff position would require citizens
of the Western countries to give up either morality or democracy on a
crucial issue, and supposedly morality and democracy are two of the primary things we wish to defend.

A criticism that especially relates to the "disproportionate threat"
type of bluff is that it initates an uncapped spiral of threatened violence.
Ramsey says that because the threats are proportioned to the prevention or
escalation of war, with all of its great evils, the threats "may justifiably go quite high".[30] But of course, such threats themselves make it
appear that any actual war will be that much worse.[31] Therefore the enemy
is justified in making even greater threats, and the cycle continues.
The only limit to this rising spiral is that the threat must be credible.
At whatever point the process stops, there is always a risk that the threat
will be carried out. Even if one side is able to sustain its bluff and
not execute its threat in a moment of crisis, the other side may act on
the threat; thus a nation's own bluff may increase the amount of destruction it suffers.

Of course, this involves many strategic and moral considerations about
what kind of deterrent is most effective and whether emphasis should be
placed on preventing or limiting war. But even apart from these questions,

---

[30] Ramsey, Peace, Churches, Bomb, p. 56.

[31] Cf. Theodore Weber, Modern War and the Pursuit of Peace, p. 15:
"The deterrent willed into action is self-contradictory: it draws upon
the home base destruction greater than that which would have occurred had
there been no deterrent."

a willingness to engage in the spiral of threats prevents honesty and integrity in openly promoting one's values and commitments, whether on the personal, national, or ecclesiastic levels. It requires citizens and military/political leaders to say to each other--or rather to think of each other--in regard to these threats: "I trust that you are honorable, therefore you must be lying." The cost to integrity is lessened a bit by openly declaring, as does J. Bryan Hehir, that one is only bluffing, but then the effectiveness of the deterrent is reduced. One is still left with paying a high price for a very risky venture. And the bluff position, particularly when it is not openly acknowledged, undermines itself. Nuclear pacifists are right to question whether, when we keep claiming that our security depends upon nuclear weapons and keep threatening to use them immorally if necessary, we would actually have enough restraint in a moment of crisis not to so use them.

Some of the proponents of the bluff position (as well as some who hold the counterforce position but are uncomfortable with it) adopt it as a temporary necessity. They hope that international law and world government will be able to overcome the moral (and strategic) dilemmas of the nuclear age. First we must ask how long such an interim is likely to be. The years since the advent of nuclear weapons have stretched into decades and still there is little progress toward these goals. If anything nuclear weapons have shown the weakness of international law, for there has been little effort to regulate or prohibit the use of nuclear weapons, although there have been test-ban and non-proliferation treaties. Also, far from being able to rescue morality, international law needs to

be corrected by morality since it assumes the right of reprisals,[32] which
at least in some forms is condemned by bluff and counterforce proponents
alike. Also, both international law and world authority have been hindered
by the assumptions that national sovereignty cannot be surrendered and
that any means--including nuclear weapons--may be used to protect it. The
bluff theory only reinforces those assumptions, though in a mild form when
the position is stated openly. Furthermore, the bluff position undermines
the honesty which is a basic ingredient of any trust between nations, and
such trust is necessary if international cooperation and world authority
is to be in any way advanced.

The American bishops (through 1979) have stretched the bluff position
as far as it will go--and farther than it will go. It is doubtful that
there is as much difference between the "possession" of nuclear weapons and
the threat to use them as Cardinal Krol seems to believe. A nuclear
arsenal cannot be "possessed" in the same way that Great Grandfather's
old shotgun can be hung on the wall. The "possession" of nuclear weapons
requires a vast maintenance system in which thousands of people are
employed and millions of dollars are spent each day. It requires forces
to be on such a state of alert that strategic weapons could be fired in
minutes, with all of the risks of war by accident and miscalculation
which that entails. Such "possession" is certainly a threat, even if it
is not verbal, and the threat is not located in "the weapons themselves"
but in the institutions which maintain them. The bishops are concerned
about political realities, but it would be awkward indeed for a Secretary

---

[32] Gunter Levy, "Superior Orders, Nuclear Warfare, and the Dictates
of Conscience: The Dilemma of Military Obedience in the Atomic Age,"
Political Science Review, LV (1961), 19.

of Defense to try to implement their view. Presumably he would have to publicly ignore nuclear weapons altogether, which would be difficult, particularly at budget time.

The position of the bishops is understandable but untenable. In September, 1979, Cardinal Krol pointed out "the urgency of the Catholic demand that the nuclear arms race be reversed".[33] He said that if the hope of such a reversal were to disappear, "the moral attitude of the Catholic Church would almost certainly have to shift to one of uncompromising condemnation of both use _and_ possession"[34] of nuclear weapons. On behalf of most of the bishops, Cardinal Krol supported SALT II despite the fact that it was a deceleration rather than a reversal of the nuclear arms race. Since then SALT II has died, the Reagan administration has undertaken to "rearm America",[35] and more and more bishops are opposing nuclear weapons in increasingly radical ways. New U.S./Soviet negotiations are under way, but it will be some time before the results are known. The bishops have not defined a stable place to stand--the time has come for them to move forward, and they are beginning to do so. In November, 1982, the American bishops as a body will make another statement on the nuclear issue. The position they take may be significant in American and even international politics; it will certainly be very important not only for the Roman Catholic Church but for other Christian churches as well.

---

[33]Cardinal John Krol, "SALT II: A Statement of Support," _Origins_, IX (September 13, 1979), 197.

[34]Ibid.

[35]Secretary of Defense Caspar Weinberger, News Release of a speech before the Navy League of Dallas, October 7, 1981, p. 5.

The Just War Tradition and the Challenge of Nuclear Weapons

I have offered criticisms of nuclear pacifism, Paul Ramsey's counter-force theory, and the bluff position. We can now turn to ask the larger question of what new challenges modern war, and particularly nuclear war, poses to the just war tradition itself. I will discuss this question in two categories, the logic and the unity of the tradition.

In Chapter IV I based my analysis of ethical reasoning on two basic types, deontological and teleological or consequentialist. Both are employed in the just war tradition, with deontological thinking associated especially with the principle of discrimination and teleological thinking with the principle of proportionality.

The first question we might ask of the deontological aspect of just war logic is simply how firmly it can be maintained in Western culture. First of all, the deontological form of ethics seems to be losing ground in academic ethics, the church, and the culture at large. Secondly, this is happening at a time when the whole political/cultural situation is cast in a form that has always put the just war tradition to a severe test. In the medieval period when the majority of people shared some measure of a common cultural and religious heritage in "Christendom", there was a basis for calling Christian belligerents to observe common restraints. However, without this mutual ground there was a tendency to demand less restraint in dealing with the "infidel", who in turn was not trusted to observe limits. Today the confrontation between the Western and communist countries is such that for the West, the nuclear opponents are "infidels" because they subscribe to a conflicting ideology. In such a situation there is a tendency in theory and in practice to bend deontological demands.

The pressure to relax moral limits is also increased by the very fact that the nuclear powers are able to threaten each other with such swift and overwhelming destruction. Of course, nuclear pacifists and others have argued that it is irrational to seek security through nuclear weapons, but as we have seen the issue finally comes down to its basis in ultimate hope. In an increasingly pluralistic Western culture, it may prove more difficult to advocate unconditional moral demands based on Christian hope, especially if these risk or require suffering. However, the practice of Christians has been so wanting in this regard that a prior question is whether the demands of the just war tradition can be firmly held even within the church.

While the strength of deontological just war logic is a very important practical question, the advent of nuclear weapons has fostered a more basic historical and theoretical challenge to it. Richard S. Hartigan and William V. O'Brien have claimed that the principle of non-combatant immunity was a late (sixteenth and seventeenth century) addition to the just war tradition and is not an immutable principle of the natural law.[36] Historically we might ask how many just war theorists have ever placed any absolute limits on military necessity, and theoretically we might ask how a deontological principle might be grounded. Such questions are beyond the scope of this study, but since both nuclear pacifists and

---

[36] Richard Shelly Hartigan, "Non-Combatant Immunity: An Analysis of Its Philosophical and Historical Origins," (Unpublished doctoral dissertation, Georgetown University, 1964); R. S. Hartigan, "Non-Combatant Immunity: Reflections on Its Origins and Present Status," Review of Politics, XXIX (1967), 204-220; William V. O'Brien, Peace, Churches, Bomb, p. 98; W. V. O'Brien, Nuclear War, Deterrence and Morality (New York, 1967), pp. 82-86.

counterforce theorists rely so heavily on the deontological application of the principle of discrimination, they must answer this challenge.

The teleological reasoning of the principle of proportionality, despite its mathematical language, has always been extremely intuitive with hardly any guidelines.[37] How could one weigh the respective values of, for instance, the life of a soldier, the life of a child, an art museum, national sovereignty, a bridge, international justice, a natural landmark, and so forth? Also, how does one weigh the respective values of loss to one's own country, a neutral nation, and the enemy nation? Even if one could quantify such things, it has always been very difficult to judge with any accuracy what the actual military and political outcome of a war would be, not to mention its economic, moral, cultural, and religious ramifications. The development of nuclear weapons has made prediction vastly more difficult than ever. We have strategic science with its numerous scenarios, but no one knows what would actually happen in a nuclear war. Even if we knew what kind of bombs would fall where, it might not be possible to judge the effects of nuclear war, which might last for thousands of years.

Proportionality was always a gamble, but today there is a difference. Previously wars took months and years to prosecute, allowing time to evaluate the situation and, if necessary, sue for peace. A full-scale nuclear war could be over within hours or days. Entering a war used to be like a game of poker: players could look at their hands; they knew

---

[37] Joseph C. McKenna, "Ethics and War: A Catholic View," The American Political Science Review, LIV (1960), 651, says that the only criterion is that the assessment must be made in moral rather than material terms.

the odds; they could call or raise the bets; and, if the stakes became too high, they could fold. Nuclear war is like a game of Russian Roulette with some chambers of the gun containing blanks and others, live cartridges. If one pulls the trigger on a blank, he or she might suffer injury but not death; if the cartridge is live, it is the end.

The Russian Roulette character of nuclear war creates still another new problem for proportionality thinking. Counterforce theorists readily admit that no cause whatsoever would justify all-out nuclear war. They also admit that any war runs some risk of becoming all-out nuclear war. In order to avoid becoming nuclear pacifists, they are willing to accept the risk of all-out war (but not to justify ever doing it). As I noted earlier, Ramsey adopts the principle that the gravity of an event must be reduced by its probability. To put it in straight mathematical terms, we might say that if there is only a ten percent chance that a war will become all-out nuclear war, then only ten percent of the evil it would cause must be weighed into the equation when judging the proportionality of a limited war. This places an additional burden upon the criterion, for now the probability of escalation must be determined. Even apart from that, however, if all-out nuclear war is so evil that nothing can justify it, it must be assigned infinite weight in any judgment of proportionality. But in mathematics, ten percent of infinity is still infinity--in which case it would be immoral ever to risk all-out nuclear war. The only way to avoid this conclusion is to withhold the judgment of "infinity", but this again moves the argument to the level of hope and transcends the principle to proportion itself.

What I have said so far relates to weighing the consequences of actual war in the nuclear age. But nuclear deterrence also raises new

questions for the principle of proportionality. If deterrence really
were, as advocates of the bluff position maintain, a realm of action
wholly separate from warfare, then any evaluation of it would have nothing
to do with the costs and benefits of war. But if, as I have argued along
with nuclear pacifists, at least for citizens the deterrent threat must be
evaluated as an actual intention, what is threatened may be weighed
according to the principle of proportionality. In this case, however, the
costs and benefits of provisional, future war must be judged rather than
those of an actual impending war. That the two cases must be judged by
the same scale may be justified not only by the need to evaluate the
present intention of the agent in making the deterrent threat but also
by the demand for integrity on the part of the agent, the need for the
communication and promotion of one's values, respect for the role of
citizens, allies, and even opponents in shaping policy, and the need for
the credibility of the deterrent threat itself. Still, the application
of the proportionality criterion will be more difficult in the case of
deterrence because it must rely on general definitions of costs and benefits apart from any specific situation.

In these ways modern warfare, and particularly nuclear warfare,
creates new problems or exacerbates old ones in the very ways of thinking employed in the just war tradition. Difficult as these problems may
prove, there is an even more fundamental challenge to the tradition:
the nuclear debate I have described demonstrates that the assumed unity
of the just war tradition as received in this century has been shattered
by nuclear weapons.

That basic unity I take to be as follows: war undertaken by moral
means is able to be an effective form of force used to advance legitimate

political goals such as justice, security, and peace. It is assumed that since war may be lawfully undertaken it may also be lawfully threatened for political purposes. In fact it is the implicit threat of war which helps preserve those political goals even in times of peace. Also, since there is no division in what may be threatened and what may be done, there is no division in one's stated intention and one's actual intention. In short, there is a unity between politics, morality, war, the threat of war, actual intention and stated intention.

The nuclear era has caused various kinds of splits in this unity. First, the military/political situation itself revealed a split in the era of mutual assured destruction. When each society became capable of largely destroying the other, war in its maximum form was no longer able to serve national political purposes. Nevertheless, both sides continued to threaten each other with massive nuclear war. Thus the threat, as long as it was not actualized, was seen to have a useful political function. No longer were war and the threat of war for the sake of deterrence to be regarded on the same plane of political usefulness. This generated pressures to bring the two back into correspondence, but the ultimate threat of assured destruction was never withdrawn.

In terms of moral evaluation, massive nuclear retaliation is clearly immoral when judged by the just war criteria. However, those who hold the bluff position believe in the political usefulness of the deterrent threat. Therefore in order to keep morality and politics together, they absolutize the split between nuclear war and the threat of nuclear war. In the process they also make one's stated (or implied) intention independent of one's actual intention, with only the latter subject to evaluation by the just war criteria.

Nuclear pacifists argue that in order for the deterrent threats to have political utility, there must be a unity of intention between what is publicly threatened and what is actually intended, at least on the part of citizens. Thus nuclear pacifists reunite the public and private aspects of intention, and in so doing they use the same moral standard to judge what may be done and what may be threatened. But of course they conclude that nuclear war is incompatible with the moral criteria of the just war tradition.

Both nuclear pacifists and those who hold the bluff position agree, then, that nuclear weapons force a departure from the way in which the just war tradition has been applied to warfare in the past. They differ in their judgments about which previous assumptions have to be rejected. Counterforce advocates are the only ones who try to hold all of the traditional just war elements together: morality, politics, war, the threat of war, stated intentions and actual intention. They do this by insisting that limited nuclear war directed against military targets can both serve national political purposes and meet the demands of morality. Thus there is no need to evaluate differently war which is contemplated and war which is threatened, or actual and apparent intention.

However, in order to maintain the unity of the just war tradition, counterforce advocates have stretched its elements as far as possible. Earlier in this chapter I questioned whether even counterforce nuclear war could pass a close scrutiny of the criteria of discrimination and proportionality. I also questioned whether in Paul Ramsey's position the needs of deterrence were not actually governing intention rather than the needs of fighting a nuclear war. In fact the tendency to split apparent intention from actual intention, the deterrent threat from actual war, was manifested when Ramsey supplemented, or rather abandoned, the counter-force position for the deterrent bluff. Even apart from this, however, I believe that Ramsey stretched the just war theory not only to but beyond its breaking point in an effort to make it fit nuclear war, even counter-force nuclear war.

In the end, though, it is Dr. Ramsey himself who finally demonstrates that the old assumptions are outdated, even if he does not recognize the fact. By 1972, when he wrote "The MAD Nuclear Policy" (Worldview, XV, 16-20), Ramsey had abandoned the counter-city bluff position (p. 18). He also withdrew the term counterforce deterrent (type A), because it implied a focus on the nuclear forces of the enemy (p. 17). Instead he would prefer, if feasible, a countercombatant deterrent as suggested by the analysts Arthur Lee Burns and Bruce M. Russett. Burns suggested that rather than making millions of noncombatants hostages as in the MAD deterrence policy, we threaten to retaliate against armed forces only, such as whole armies and some nuclear forces, as a way of threatening the continued existence of the Soviet or Chinese regimes (p. 17). Along the same lines Russett suggested that the ability of the Soviet Union to defend itself against its neighbors be threatened. In particular, Soviet forces and bases along the Chinese border would be destroyed, making Russia vulnerable to China (p. 17).

This scheme does remove civilian populations from the status of direct hostages, though it makes them indirect hostages to political domination. However, the deterring effect of this countercombatant threat is not based on the ability and intent to wage war, for such an attack would not be an act of war at all. War in just war theory is the use of force to repel and overcome the hostile forces by which one is actually threatened. Thus

Ramsey says in War and the Christian Conscience that one may "never directly or intentionally bring about the death of any man not engaged or closely co-operating in the hostile force that he must and in justice should repel" (p. 270). But the just war tradition of recent times has never assumed that all soldiers, or even all soldiers in uniform, were combatants. Those on leave, sick, wounded, or captured cannot be killed because they are not at that time contributing to the hostile exercise of force by the opposing nation. Similarly, soldiers involved in defending the border against the Chinese or serving to maintain control over the East European socialist countries are not, by the very logic of the countercombatant theory, free to contribute to the use of force against, for example, the United States. In effect this theory simply holds hundreds of thousands or even millions of inactive soldiers hostage, rather than tens of millions of civilians. It threatens military forces but not, first of all, combatants, so the term "countercombatant" is misleading.

The type of deterrence Ramsey finally endorses--pending the judgment of others about its feasibility--poses a threat based on the use of force but not on the ability and willingness to engage in combat. One threatens to hurt the enemy nation in retaliation, but not to resist and defeat its forces. Here the logic of deterrence is clearly severed from the logic of war, and military power is used in a contest of wills, not strength--a situation which Ramsey earlier deplored (Just War, pp. 221-225). This no doubt reflects the fact that strategic nuclear war can no longer fit the old model of combat because in the use of strategic force there is no front line, not enough of the enemy's forces can be destroyed to prevent the enemy from being able to do massive harm, and even if this could be done it would be immoral by just war standards. Apparently Ramsey no longer attempts to base nuclear deterrence on (strategic) nuclear war because in any likely form it can no longer serve a useful political purpose. (Neither, as I argued above, can extensive tactical nuclear war.)

If nuclear war is no longer combat and cannot serve politics, then the heart of the counterforce position has been cut out,[38] and the counterforce position is the only one which tries to maintain the traditional unity of the just war theory. All just war theorists, whether they acknowledge it or not, must now reject some assumptions of the old synthesis.

Since nuclear weapons have brought the world as a whole to a point of crisis, it is not surprising that they have deeply challenged the just war tradition. I have argued that the tradition shows the most rigor and integrity in those who reject the use and possession of nuclear weapons. But it remains to be seen whether and in what form the just war tradition-- or the world itself--will survive the nuclear challenge. Be that as it may, the present era does hold one advantage for the Christian churches. Perhaps now more than at any time in the past 17 centuries many Christians are being driven to a deep examination of their old assumptions, and to ask once again what it means to follow the Prince of Peace in service to a violent world.

---

[38]In complaining that Walter Stein is more of a pacifist than a nuclear pacifist, Ramsey remarks that "The principles and limits and tests of the just war which were erected on the understanding that force and politics and morality are connected (and which can certainly be used in the justification and limitation of systems of graduated deterrence) must be annulled..." if, as Stein says, nuclear war and deterrent threat are always driven to the uppermost levels of violence. Ramsey, Just War, p. 346. I am arguing here that even striving for the lowermost levels of violence as the countercombatant theory does show that force (i.e. war), politics, and morality are not connected when it comes to nuclear weapons.

Appendix

OTHER EXAMPLES OF NUCLEAR PACIFISM

Except for my discussion of the Roman Catholic hierarchy and the
World Council of Churches in Chapter I, in this dissertation I have dealt
only with individual authors from the United States and Great Britain.
I would here like to offer a couple of examples which illustrate that
nuclear pacifism occurs in other countries and that it may assume
ecclesiastical/political significance. I will briefly refer first to the
Reformed Churches of the Netherlands. There are of course many other
cases of nuclear pacifism, particularly in Europe.

Karl Barth and Helmut Gollwitzer

It is generally known that Karl Barth supported the Allied cause
in World War II. Less noted is his statement in volume III/4 of the
Church Dogmatics that "the inflexible negative of pacifism has almost
infinite arguments in its favor and is almost overpoweringly strong."[1]
Still less widely known is the fact that Barth was a nuclear pacifist.
This is due in large part to the fact that he expressed this view more in
personal letters and pamphlets and other political activity than in writings
for a wide audience.[2] In the Church Dogmatics Barth made only one passing

---

[1]Karl Barth, Church Dogmatics, III/4, ed. G. W. Bromiley and T. F.
Torrance (Edinburgh, 1961), p. 455.

[2]Cf. Eberhard Busch, Karl Barth, trans. John Bowden (Philadelphia,
1976), pp. 381-386, 430-435.

reference to nuclear weapons. However, in the 1950's he opposed the atomic armament of Switzerland and the rearmament of Germany, particularly with nuclear weapons. John Howard Yoder has documented Barth's total support for the movement within the Evangelical Church in Germany to declare that Christians cannot "participate in the design, testing, manu- facturing, stocking and use of atomic weapons, nor in training with these weapons".[3] The statement went on to claim that approval or neutrality in the face of preparations for atomic war is a denial of the Christian faith.

Barth's nuclear pacifism occurred in the context of his general refusal to contribute to the East/West confrontation by condemning the Communists. In looking at the Eastern point of view he said:

> Did we give the Eastern partner any choice? Did we not provoke him by erecting a massive Western defense alliance, by encircling him with artillery, by establishing the German Federal Republic--which seemed to him like a clenched fist pushed under his nose--and by rearming this republic and equipping it with nuclear missiles? Did we not challenge our former partner to cor- responding countermeasures of power display and thus in no small measure strengthen him in his peculiar malice? Did the West finally know no better counsel than to put its trust in its in- famous A- and H-bombs? And did it not serve the West right to have to realize that the other side had not remained idle in regard to such weapons?[4]

---

[3] John Howard Yoder, <u>Karl Barth and the Problem of War</u> (Nashville and New York, 1970), p. 135.

[4] Karl Barth, "Recapitulation Number Three," <u>The Christian Century</u>, LXXVII (1960), 73.

For this stance Barth suffered a great deal of criticism, much of it harsh, but he never altered his position.[5]

While Karl Barth wrote little about nuclear weapons, his friend and former pupil Helmut Gollwitzer did write more extensively about the subject. Already in 1957 he laid out a full nuclear pacifist position using many of the arguments which came to be common.[6] I referred to him briefly in Chapter II. Like Barth, Gollwitzer urged dialogue and the building of peace with the Eastern bloc. He saw nuclear war as a greater threat to the West than were the Russians. Gollwitzer can speak with authority because for several years during and after World War II he was a prisoner of war in the Soviet Union.

The Reformed Churches of the Netherlands

The major Reformed Churches in the Netherlands have long taken a strong stand against nuclear weapons. The General Synod of the Dutch Reformed Church (Hervormde Kerk) stated in 1962 that, "It is our opinion after having taken account of the completely peculiar and exceptional character of atomic weapons...that they cannot be considered as genuine weapons because they are in every possible case unusable to reach any possible goal for the sake of which the force of weapons may legitimately be applied." Therefore the Synod concluded that, "On the basis of what we said about the peace-making task of the church and the nature of atomic weapons, the church cannot do otherwise than to pronounce a radical no

---

[5] Ibid., pp. 73-74. Cf. also Busch, op. cit.

[6] Helmut Gollwitzer, Die Christen und die Atomwaffen, Theologische Existenz Heute, Nr. 61 (München, 1957). Cf. also Helmut Gollwitzer, "Christian Commitment," Therefore Choose Life (London, 1961), pp. 32-41; Helmut Gollwitzer, "Votum zur Frage Krieg und Frieden," Junge Kirche, XXVII (1966), 435-441.

against atomic weapons."[7] While the 1962 statement of the Synod radically opposed any use of nuclear weapons, it gave only qualified opposition to their possession. In 1979 the Synod carried the discussion further by focusing on the question of whether even the possession of nuclear weapons could be morally justified. It issued a booklet entitled Kernbewapening (Nuclear Armament)[8] for general discussion in the individual churches, preparatory to a later statement by the Synod. In November, 1980 the Synod condemned the possession of nuclear weapons and, in view of the past failure of multilateral measures, called for the unilateral de-nuclearization of the Netherlands.[9]

Another major Reformed Church in the Netherlands, the Gerevormeerde Kerk, has also discussed the issue. For instance, in response to the issue of the neutron bomb, the Synod of the Gerevormeerde Kerk spoke in 1978 of "the demonic nature of weapons and strategies of mass destruction, and of the arms race itself." It declared that "all Christians can be expected to take measures toward extricating themselves from the false salvation of atomic weapons, and moving closer to the way and truth of Jesus Christ," which includes "making efforts particularly toward the abolishment of means of mass destruction."[10] However, in the interest of

---

[7] Generale Synode van de Nederlandse Hervormde Kerk, Het Vraagstuk van de Kernwapenen ('s-Gravenhage, 1962). Translation by John Howard Yoder. Italics in original.

[8] Generale Synode van de Nederlandse Hervormde Kerk, Kernbewapening (s-Gravenhage, 1979).

[9] "Hope against Hope in the Nuclear Age." The Ecumenical Review, July, 1981, pp. 249-256.

[10] Synode van de Gerevormeerde Kerk te Zwalle, "Kernbewapening," Kerkinformatie, May, 1978. Translation by Joel Cooper.

unity the Synod did not specify any particular actions, such as an
endorsement of unilateral disarmament, except for opposing the neutron
bomb.

Both the Hervormde and the Gerevormeerde churches are members of the
Interchurch Peace Council (Interkerkelijk Vredesberaad, IKV) which was
started in 1966 by the Protestant and Catholic churches of the Netherlands.
The Council in 1977 started a campaign to obtain government condemnation
of all nuclear weapons. Its slogan was, "Help rid the world of nuclear
weapons--let it begin in the Netherlands." With the help of others such
as members of the Communist Party, the IKV has played a key role in gal-
vanizing and co-ordinating current Dutch opposition to NATO's deployment
of new Pershing II and cruise nuclear missiles. The Dutch movement as a
whole and the IKV in particular have been instrumental in leading European
opposition to nuclear weapons, which is currently a political force of
international significance.

SELECTED BIBLIOGRAPHY*

Allers, Ulrich S. and O'Brien, William V. (eds.). Christian Ethics and
    Nuclear Warfare. Washington, D.C.: Institute of World Polity,
    Georgetown University, 1963.

Anscombe, G. E. M. (Elizabeth). "War and Murder." In Nuclear Weapons
    and Christian Conscience, pp. 45-62. Edited by Walter Stein.
    London: Merlin Press, 1961.

Bennett, John C. (ed.). Nuclear Weapons and the Conflict of Conscience.
    New York: Charles Scribner's Sons, 1962.

Bloesch, Donald G. "The Christian and the Drift Towards War," Theology
    and Life, II (1959), 318-326.

Christian Approach to Nuclear War, A. New York: Church Peace Mission,
    [1960]. Reprinted in Worldview, IV (1961), 3-7.

Clancy, William (ed.). The Moral Dilemma of Nuclear Weapons: Essays from
    Worldview. New York: The Council on Religion and International
    Affairs, 1961.

Crane, Paul. "Catholics and Nuclear War," The Month, New Series, XXII
    (1959), 223-229.

Dougherty, James E. "The Christian and Nuclear Pacifism," Catholic World,
    CXCVIII (1964), 336-346.

Dulles, John Foster. "Policy for Security and Peace," Foreign Affairs,
    XXXII (1954), 353-364.

Fey, Harold E. "Fifteen Years in Hell is Enough," Christian Century
    LXXVII (1960), 891-892.

Finn, James (ed.). Peace, the Churches and the Bomb. New York: The
    Council on Religion and International Affairs, 1965.

Ford, Harold P. and Winters, Francis X. (eds.). Ethics and Nuclear Strategy?
    Maryknoll, N.Y.: Orbis Books, 1977.

Ford, John C. "The Hydrogen Bombing of Cities," Theology Digest, XVIII
    (1957), 6-9.

_____

*Some important articles are listed separately even though the books
in which they appear are also listed.

Ford, John C. "The Morality of Obliteration Bombing," <u>Theological Studies</u>, V (1944), 261-309.

Gessert, Robert A. "P. D. 59: The Better Way," <u>Worldview</u>, November, 1980, pp. 7-9.

_____, and Hehir, J. Bryan. <u>The New Nuclear Debate</u>. Special Studies No. 215. New York: The Council on Religion and International Affairs, 1976.

Gollwitzer, Helmut. "Christian Commitment." In <u>Therefore Choose Life</u>: <u>Essays on the Nuclear Crisis</u>, pp. 32-41. London: The International Fellowship of Reconciliation, 1961.

Gottwald, Norman K. "Moral and Strategic Reflections on the Nuclear Dilemma," <u>Christianity and Crisis</u>, XXI (1962), 239-242.

_____. "Nuclear Realism or Nuclear Pacifism?," <u>Christian Century</u>, LXXVII (1960), 895-899.

Hehir, J. Bryan. "The Just-War Ethic and Catholic Theology: Dynamics of Change and Continuity." In <u>War or Peace? The Search for New Answers</u>, pp. 15-39. Edited by Thomas A. Shannon. Maryknoll, N.Y.: Orbis Books, 1980.

_____. "P. D. 59: New Issue in an Old Argument," <u>Worldview</u>, November, 1980, pp. 10-12.

Kennan, George F. "Foreign Policy and Christian Conscience." Address at Princeton Theological Seminary. <u>Atlantic Monthly</u>, CCIII (1959), 44-49. Reprinted in <u>The Moral Dilemma of Nuclear Weapons: Essays from Worldview</u>. Edited by William Clancy. New York: The Council on Religion and International Affairs, 1961, pp. 69-78.

Krol, Cardinal John. "The Churches and Nuclear War," <u>Origins</u>, IX (1979), 235-236.

_____. "SALT II: A Statement of Support," <u>Origins</u>, IX (1979-80), 195-199.

Lawler, Justus George. <u>Nuclear War: The Ethic, The Rhetoric, The Reality</u>: <u>A Catholic Assessment</u>. Westminster, Maryland: The Newman Press, 1965.

Lefever, Ernest W. "Facts, Calculation and Political Ethics." In <u>The Moral Dilemma of Nuclear Weapons</u>, pp. 38-43. Edited by William Clancy. New York: The Council on Religion and International Affairs, 1961.

McFadden, William R. "A Theological Evaluation of Nuclear Pacifism as Held by Selected Christian Thinkers." Unpublished doctoral dissertation. School of Theology, Boston University, 1966.

McKenna, Joseph C. "Ethics and War: A Catholic View," American Political Science Review, LIV (1960), 647-658.

McNamara, Robert S. "The United States and Western Europe." Address at the University of Michigan, June 16, 1962. Vital Speeches of the Day, XXVIII (1962), 626-629.

McReavy, Lawrence L. "The Debate on the Morality of Future War," Clergy Review, VL (1960), 77-87.

_____. "The Morality of Nuclear War," The Tablet (London), CCXI (March 29, 1958), 292-294.

_____. Peace and War in Catholic Doctrine. Oxford: Catholic Social Guild, 1963.

_____. "Reprisals: A Second Opinion," Clergy Review, XX (1941), 131-138.

Markus, R. A. "Conscience and Deterrence." In Nuclear Weapons and Christian Conscience, pp. 65-88. Edited by Walter Stein. London: Merlin Press, 1961.

Mohan, Robert Paul. "Thermonuclear War and the Christian." In Christian Ethics and Nuclear Warfare. Edited by Ulrich S. Allers and William V. O'Brien. Washington, D.C.: Institute of World Polity, Georgetown University, 1963.

Murray, John Courtney. Morality and Modern War. New York: The Council on Religion and International Affairs, 1959.

Nagle, William J. (ed.). Morality and Modern Warfare: The State of the Question. Baltimore: Helicon Press, 1960.

Potter. Ralph B. "The Structure of Certain American Christian Responses to the Nuclear Dilemma." Unpublished doctoral dissertation. Harvard University, 1965.

Ramsey, Paul. Again, the Justice of Deterrence. New York: The Council on Religion and International Affairs, 1965. Reprinted in Paul Ramsey, The Just War: Force and Political Responsibility. New York: Charles Scribner's Sons, 1968, pp. 314-366.

_____. "Dream and Reality in Deterrence and Defense," Christianity and Crisis, XXI (1961), 228-232.

_____. The Just War: Force and Political Responsibility. New York: Charles Scribner's Sons, 1968.

_____. The Limits of Nuclear War. New York: The Council on Religion and International Affairs, 1963. Reprinted in Paul Ramsey, The Just War: Force and Political Responsibility. New York: Charles Scribner's Sons, 1968, pp. 211-258.

Ramsey, Paul. "The MAD Nuclear Policy," Worldview, XV (1972), 16-20.

_____. "Right and Wrong Calculation," Worldview, II (1959), 6-9.
Reprinted in The Moral Dilemma of Nuclear Weapons. Edited by William
Clancy. New York: The Council on Religion and International Affairs,
1961, pp. 47-54.

_____. War and the Christian Conscience: How Shall Modern War Be
Conducted Justly? Durham, N.C.: Duke University Press, 1961.

Ryan, John K. "Modern War and Basic Ethics." Doctoral dissertation,
Catholic University of America, 1933. Published under that title at
Milwaukee: The Bruce Publishing Company, 1940.

Smedes, Lewis; Paul Steeves; Arthur Holmes; Harold Brown; Jim Wallis, and
George Mavrodes. "Rumors of Wars," Eternity, June, 1980, pp. 14-19.

Stein, Walter. Dialogue with editorials in The Tablet (London), CCXVII
(1963), 274, 302, 348, 376-377, 413-414, 436-437, 475, 491-492.

_____. (ed.). Nuclear Weapons and Christian Conscience. London:
Merlin Press, 1961. Published in the United States as Nuclear
Weapons: A Catholic Response. New York: Sheed and Ward, 1961.

_____. (ed.). Peace on Earth: The Way Ahead. London and Melbourne:
Sheed and Ward, 1966.

Theisen, Sylvester P. "Man and Nuclear Weapons," The American Benedictine
Review, XIV (1963), 365-390.

Thompson, Charles S. (ed.). Morals and Missiles: Catholic Essays on the
Problem of War Today. London: James Clarke Co. Ltd., 1959.

Walzer, Michael. Just and Unjust Wars: A Moral Argument with Historical
Illustrations. New York: Basic Books, Inc., 1977.

Wasserstrom, Richard. "On the Morality of War: A Preliminary Inquiry."
In War and Morality, pp. 78-101. Edited by Richard Wasserstrom.
Belmont, Calif.: Wadsworth Publishing Company, Inc., 1970.

Watkin, E. I. "Unjustifiable War." In Morals and Missiles: Catholic
Essays on the Problem of War Today, pp. 51-52. Edited by Charles
Thompson. London: James Clarke & Co., Ltd., 1959.

Weber, Theodore. Modern War and the Pursuit of Peace. New York: The
Council on Religion and International Affairs, 1968.

Winters, Francis X. "The Bow or the Cloud? American Bishops Challenge the
Arms Race," America, CLV (July 18-25, 1981), 26-30.